jali

jali

oliver twist

EBURY
PRESS

EBURY PRESS

UK | USA | Canada | Ireland | Australia
India | New Zealand | South Africa | China

Ebury Press is part of the Penguin Random House group of companies
whose addresses can be found at global.penguinrandomhouse.com.

Penguin
Random House
Australia

First published by Ebury Press 2023

Front cover photograph by Kiera Chevell
Back cover photograph by Tom Gilligan
Cover design by Alex Ross © Penguin Random House Australia Pty Ltd
Internal design by Midland Typesetters, Australia
Typeset in 13/18.5 pt Adobe Garamond Pro by Midland Typesetters

Printed and bound in Australia by Griffin Press, an accredited
ISO AS/NZS 14001 Environmental Management Systems printer

A catalogue record for this
book is available from the
National Library of Australia

ISBN 978 1 76104 753 4

penguin.com.au

We at Penguin Random House Australia acknowledge that Aboriginal and Torres
Strait Islander peoples are the Traditional Custodians and the first storytellers
of the lands on which we live and work. We honour Aboriginal and Torres
Strait Islander peoples' continuous connection to Country, waters, skies and
communities. We celebrate Aboriginal and Torres Strait Islander stories, traditions
and living cultures; and we pay our respects to Elders past and present.

we do not meet on the dance floor,
yet we dance in the glow,
you take two steps backwards,
I take two steps forwards,

moving with flow same way flowers open to the sun
unfolding to make clear the picture of our sum
you are sweet like the Venezuelan rum
my heart beats for you like the Nigerian drum

with you I hear the music differently,
around you I dance differently,
we do not meet on the dance floor,
yet here we are,

you are melody to my tune
you smile as I press play
dance with me, my love
before the music changes

To Sahar

'Been trying to be very honest. Because my whole life was shrouded in secrets. And I figured the only route I haven't tried was the truth. So I am saying everything, here is everything.'

'Rothaniel'—Jerrod Carmichael

I

Ngomas are playing on a clear sky night. Full moon is out. The bright light hitting the surface of Lake Kivu is shining. People dancing while the ngomas emit music and beautiful girls sing melodies in my mother tongue, Kinyarwanda. Sounding so good, makes you want to join in. One girl singing is wearing a gorgeous dark-red dress in flowery patterns made from Chitenje, a fabric common in central Africa. Her arms wave above her head as she is dancing. In front of her is this young man dancing with her. He is wearing a dark-blue long-sleeve shirt with black trousers.

This is how I imagine my father meeting my mother. He is nervous around her when they dance. He is probably thinking, 'She must cost five cows and five goats.' While this is a frugal way to think of my mother, it is also a great compliment. Five cows and five goats in today's language means my mother is a babe, ten out of ten. Her skin is flawless, her jaw and hair matchless.

I get most of my looks from my mother, of course—dark eyes, smooth skin and great black hair. The similarity is uncanny. On a suspect line-up, you could not set us apart. You cannot see it here while my father is dancing with my mother, but he will start going bald in the future. This will give him a striking look, and he will not like it. Neither will my mother. Every night before I go to bed, I cross my fingers that the next morning I wake up with a full head of hair.

My mother and father linger in their beautiful delight. I imagine, albeit of my own accord, this is the night that produced me. And as far as impactful nights that birthed me—one particular night springs to mind: 300 kilometres from Lake Kivu, something is about to happen, something hideous.

In Kigali, Rwanda, a plane carrying the presidents of Rwanda and Burundi is shot down. It plummets as quickly as extremists lift their machetes. One hundred days of relentless nightmares follow, targeting Tutsis and some Hutus. A defining genocide that leaves terror's footprints on every doorstep.

This happens in April when it rains. This rainy season, water washes blood in the streets. In every corner of the country. Beauty and ugliness, inextricably intertwined. After the death of the Rwandan president, things fall apart.

The division between Hutu and Tutsi is deadly. My father is Hutu; my mother is Tutsi. They should not be together.

Following the genocide, my parents are still in hiding. Yet I am born shortly after this time. So, while there is civil war going on, my parents are also thinking, 'But we are horny!' Soon after me, my sister Angel is born. Again, my parents are very horny during this time.

We flee from Rwanda, ending up in Dzaleka refugee camp, in the southeast of Malawi, in the Dowa district. There is a sadness about our departure. I am saying farewell to my mother tongue, Kinyarwanda. I want to say goodbye in Kinyarwanda. I want to say I will miss home in Kinyarwanda.

I want to visit every corner of my birthplace in Cyangugu. I want to swim in Lake Kivu. I want to celebrate my culture and my people before they move on without me. I want photos of my family at our home in Kigali. The beautiful home where Grandpa and Grandma laughed at photos of me as a very chubby baby. I want all these memories and images, however sentimental.

All these wishes I want will not happen. Because I am on a bus right this moment to seek refuge. Imagine you had to abandon your home at four years old. That's how flimsy life is. You could be on this bus. Being driven in the middle of the night with all kinds of civil wars around you. The bus will not make any stops because it's too dangerous to do so. You look at your parents' faces. You see how petrified they are. You cannot find the words to say goodbye to your home. You sit there in silence, taking in every image of your home for the last time.

I have found myself in my mother's kitchen, in a typical Queenslander house, built off the ground to protect it from extreme weather. Classic Australian thinking. The Northern Territory is notoriously known for this. I mean, people live underground in some of these places. But now we are in Ipswich and above ground. The timber floors in my mother's house are squeaky and loud as I tiptoe around, peering in cupboards for a way to make myself something to eat while trying not to wake up my family. They go to sleep as early as 6 pm, as if we are still in Africa.

My snooping rewards me with a cabinet full of spices, African spices. Something I cannot eat straight away, but the memories come rushing as soon as I spot them. I instantly remember my mother's kitchen being filled with spice mists and her rules around the kitchen, one of which is to never mix spices. For instance, a Rwandan dish must be filled with pure Rwandan spices, no Indian or Nigerian spices. With spices, she is a supporter of segregation. She also does not like being limited to what she can cook in the kitchen. And there has been a loss of ingredients and spice usage since I became a vegetarian. So now, she will make a beautiful plantain dish from banana—Igitoki, as it's called in my mother tongue—but all the while she grumbles, 'It is a very plain dish if you ask me.' Being a vegetarian to most of my African kinfolk, including my mother, is a phase they hope I recover from very soon.

I close my eyes and float away, back to being a small boy in the kitchen with her in Malawi, smelling the food as she cooks, my helping hand purely guided by her instructions. I am hovering from dish to dish. I can even imagine her world before she was labelled a Tutsi woman who marries a Hutu man in an African Shakespearean lethal feudal union. She has five sisters and one brother. And I know, having sisters for siblings, much is expected of them. To marry right—whatever that means. To take care of your husband and children—whatever that means. As if these are the only offerings expected from our mothers and sisters. This beautiful woman has spent so much time in the kitchen. But in another habitat of a Higgs particle, she is not only in the kitchen, she is also a queen to be loved and respected. Yes indeed, in another timeline, another time before colonialism. My mother is a queen, and me, her son, a king.

We are transported to another universe altogether when my family and I float across Lake Kivu from Cyangugu on a journey to safety. 'Oli, you were such a sea-sickness baby,' my mother later recalls in a tone of voice that is both endearing and comical—that soothing tone reserved for weather forecasters. 'You cried and vomited on board,' she says, and I am embarrassed when she shares these stories with her friends, stretching them like the muse goddess of epic poetry. Stacked together, they make a great story, but as an adult I wonder why she tells these stories in this manner—stylistically, like an in-vogue magazine editor, omitting painful parts.

I should pray that none of you get to experience this pain. This nagging continuous pain of the mind and body. Given time of a different kind, I could elaborate on my country's genocide, the painful past—its tremendous loss of a generation of my people. Fuelled by political agendas that won't hold value when it's all said and done. I am not yet born during the famous genocide in 1994 and yet when I enter the world, I will feel the full effects of this hundred-day killing spree in which close to one million Tutsis and some Hutus are slaughtered by Hutu extremists. My Hutu father opted out of killing his Tutsi wife. My family did not take part in murdering their neighbours, their teachers and fellow citizens, but when Tutsi soldier Paul Kagame becomes the president of Rwanda almost immediately after the war, all Hutus are forced to go on the run. The air full of vengeance, we must, amid turmoil, seek refuge in neighbouring countries.

Which one, though? Congo and Uganda are both at war of similar nature and form. All safety is an illusion. Each member of my family eventually realises this very truth. We cannot stay anywhere for long, and I am disoriented. Time is stretched out as I pass through it and I remember things differently, years mixed up. Please forgive me, I hope I don't get these stories mixed up. I am going from language to language. From Kinyarwanda to Swahili, and later to Chichewa and then English. Slowly my mother tongue escapes me.

It takes my family weeks to escape Rwanda and cross into Tanzania. I am four or five years old when I launch these land invasions—a journey to safety, my sister Angel and I are too young to understand the enormity of our situation, marching across national lines and plunging into peril.

In Tanzania, our first refuge, we live in Dar es Salaam temporarily, as all immigrants and refugees do, momentarily house-sitting. Sitting waiting for a house. Dar es Salaam is beautiful, but the beauty is seasonal, as if we are wealthy people chasing summer, never living in winter. I never experience the cold, the pain. I am a traveller, through time, going over time itself. My time is now, hope is for suckers. I am not one. Not me.

We move into a massive complex of apartments set off the main road. A grey, prison-like cement wall surrounds rows of houses built before independence was achieved in Tanzania, with multiple lofts stacked together like housing projects. Making my way in, I marvel at the maze, feeling a little dazed. I can't imagine someone having this much fortune, owning this much land. I have seen nothing like it before.

The property is easy to spot with its bright burgundy steel gate. A door opens into a corridor to a wide-open flat area. Apartments face each other to form a square yard in the middle, a playground—or perhaps a boxing ring. Baba Musa, who is the landlord, is a giant mountain of a man. I get to know his son, Musa, and we play together all the time, games like Phada (African hopscotch) or hide and seek—we have the most fun together. They are a well-to-do family and Musa's house has a carefully curated living room and kitchen, pastel colours everywhere, a sweet vision. If my family were this lucky to own such a house, I would never leave. I hear stories we own some land back in Rwanda, but that is in the past, and the new regime has won the war and we, my Hutu family, have lost. It's no use crying over spilt milk. We trudge forward.

I end up becoming wonderful friends with Musa. He is the type of friend you get into trouble with and get punished with. The beatings are less painful when we are in it together. My father, Seba, and his father get along well. Too well—to a point that they tag team each other when whipping us. If Musa or I get in trouble and my father is not here to punish us, his father will take over like a twisted game of relay-race whopping. Musa and I prefer beatings from my father though. His father, being a giant, whips us with a young Mike-Tyson-strength punch, a full-body-weight knockout.

My father has work in Dar es Salaam, but I don't know where. He comes home with not enough money. I see him mainly at night when he knocks off and briefly in the morning before I leave for school. My memories of school in Tanzania are punctured by poverty. My parents, consumed with their own drama, leave me to my thoughts. They know we are leaving soon, mindlessly they plan, without my knowledge. I learn at school, but it does not stick and at home I am told by my parents to say we are not residents because otherwise UNHCR will say we are not qualified to put in a resettlement application later in Malawi. It is spectacularly peculiar to keep secrets as a child—I later dedicate a good deal of time in therapy to just that: things unsaid.

Musa and I spend a lot of time getting into wonderful thrills—the kind that would make a perfect ad for a sporting, outdoor brand like Patagonia. Look at us in the air. Jumping fences, jumping fences with wires, jumping anything. Jumping, training for a military coup. We are the bravest, there is a tomorrow, and we are building it. Me and Musa. Musa and I. Our bromance beats any kind of courtship, show me any bromance better, I will wait. They should build statues out of our heroism, our adventures, our conquests, and place the statues alongside the greats in Cairo or Rome.

Musa does not know why I am here in Tanzania or how long I will be here for. I want to tell him, but I cannot.

I don't know either. Our friendship is rushed. When we are not on an adventure, we spend time in his living room, playing games, time travelling, betting on outcomes, gambling with destiny. And I watch a film—*The Gods Must Be Crazy*—for the first time on his father's massive eighties TV. At the time I think it's a great African film; only later I find out that it was in fact made by a white South African, and then my sentiment turns to: mmm, I don't trust these kinds of Africans.

Musa and I have an agreement that we will stay playful like the children in the film. We decide to hijack a motorbike belonging to the neighbour in our compound. Today I have a permanent scar on my left leg—a sharp 10-centimetre-long shiny brown mark—as a reminder of this unique high-stakes mission. On the day of, after considerable hours debating who would ride the bike first and for how long, we launch the plan. While the bike is lying idle with keys in the ignition, we approach tentatively—ninja style. Us being ninjas, we have trained for this as well. We are modern-day ordained knights; medals will dangle from our respective jackets, years from this event. I am six years old and have never ridden a motorbike before but that is not important, I will access innately all knowledge of this skill.

I jump on the bike to ignite it, but I am over-matched by the weight of it, and I fall. Neither my fall nor the weight of the bike is accounted for in my blueprint and, halfway down, I see my life flash before my eyes. I get to the ground first and then the bike gets right on top of me. It's as if I am losing my virginity, missionary style.

Once my short life reel flashing in front of me has run its brief course, instinct kicks in and I move my body, but my leg gets caught in the bike's thick greasy chain. Trying to free myself, I make it worse. I am burning. The engine grilling my skin is excruciating. I cry out like a screaming witch, alerting everyone around to my situation and sending Musa racing to fetch my mother. She rushes me to a clinic where I get patched with a bandage.

When we get home, Musa is stoked for me. I am stoked, too. We will try again when I have recovered because we will never give up. Our parents, in a display of what I can only assume is respect for our bravery, decide not to give us any beatings, but we are grounded for weeks, during which I must not see Musa or get up to more trouble.

Angel is too young to go to school but not too young to get into trouble with Musa and me, though whips are spared for her. She is a girl, so Musa and I do the fun stuff without her. She is usually stationed to be the lookout unless we play Phada, which she's allowed to join in on. But the game benefits the tallest of us, which is me—I win all the time.

Arriving home from school wearing my Kiwi polished black shoes that are now dirty because of my long walking journey, I stop and hang with the Masai at kiosks in front of our gate. I don't know Kiswahili, but I throw in a fresh word I've picked up at school—they like that I am trying to learn the language. They seem so cool and carefree. I really love this about them—they know who they are. I want in. They wear colourful Jesus gowns, usually covering only one shoulder, their bodies slender and marked with scars, tattoos and piercings. It seems not vain but vital. And their jewels are so good. Every time they see me, they lift me up to put me on their shoulders—I stand tall to look at the pretty blue skies of Dar es Salaam. I feel invincible, a giant like Goliath.

The Masai and I chat a lot about everything. We form this gang of some sort. They don't tell stories, it's kind of meaningless to them. Their traditional markings and piercings are journeys into who they are and how they discuss matters of heart. It's a show for them, they know it more than I do. I doubt they care who I am. In fact, I know they don't. It's beautiful here in my brief stay and I feel connected to this place. I can't explain it. The Masai tell me of a town called Moshi near Mount Kilimanjaro where they come from, and I want to see it with them. I see hope in their vacation eyes.

The Masai are everywhere—at the markets, near the church and mosque. It's their lifestyle to move from place to place, something we seem to have in common. Their hair attests to it—they wear it loose-goose Rastafarian style, and sometimes no hair at all, just bald, both men and women. It is beautiful. At the fresh-fruits markets, they waltz past my mother and me, nodding at me with their flexible giraffe-like necks. The ground bows to their commands as they march on it, often barefoot. They are one with their earth. For them there are no citizens or borders, just people of certain tribal principles living in a place. I watch them walk, watch them dream, watch them fly over me.

One nice sunny Saturday, I go with my mother to pick up some fresh produce at the markets. She loves markets, my mother, and I accompany her always. I see a woman selling coconuts and I try to get my mother's attention. She kneels to hear what I'm fussing about, and I bring my face to her eye level and ask her if I can have a coconut. I love coconuts, specifically the water inside, so sweet. I can close my eyes and taste it, the sweetness a reminder of the fertile soil I walked on.

Walking back home, we pass by the Masai, who have gathered under a huge tea billboard, and their expression is quite simple, the meaning behind their gaze: I am intruding here on their land, it seems. I hold tight to the bag of groceries and keep walking. 'Jambo,' they say, and we keep going, my mother and I. She doesn't know I am a member of their gang. She is embarrassing me, I think to myself. When we reach the gate, my mother opens it wide, and we walk to our house. Outside the front door a pot of water is boiling on a charcoal stove for dinner. It will be rice and beans again tonight.

Apart from my friendship with Musa or the Masai, I am lonely. I can't get too invested in relationships of any kind, knowing my departure and demise are around the corner, and it makes me sad. I want to get invested, be involved, make friends as if they will be in my life forever. Tanzania is a kind of waiting room. I don't know the xenophobia waiting for me on the other side, outside this room, in Malawi, or that my innocence will meekly exit through the window, lifting off the ground like dust, thrust into clouds by gusts. I know we have fled a dreadful situation. Part of my malaise is not having any power to change it. 'Oh God, grant me serenity to accept the things I cannot change, courage to change the things I can and wisdom to know the difference.'

In Tanzania, people use kerosene to light appliances, so it's not uncommon that my parents keep kerosene in a Sprite bottle near the stove. They will re-evaluate this choice quickly because of what I am about to do. I am about to drink kerosene. I did not know at the time of consumption that my dear beloved Sprite bottle had kerosene in it. They will snatch a full bottle of kerosene from my hands, my lips around the bottle tip.

With my jaw dropping, saliva dripping, I head towards that beacon of promise that my thirst will be quenched. Each step becoming more dramatic, as if I am a soldier determined not to leave anyone behind—crawling, slouching in high spirits. I love Sprite! I grab the bottle with zest, my tiny child fingers perfectly fitting into the small indentations in the plastic. I take a few gulps before it is snatched away from me by my mother. The aftertaste of sour is written all over my face as I realise this is not Sprite—it may be the devil's piss, but not Sprite. I smell chemicals on me now, not knowing what it is or that I am a lit match away from becoming a walking stuntman on fire.

With lightning speed, my mother grabs me and gives me some milk, which is supposed to help, but the kerosene in my body sends me into a frenzy.

Flash, flash—spaced out, my eyes opening and closing. We are in a hospital.

The hospital lines are awfully long, and my mother knows my life is on the line. She is prepared to bribe someone, bribe anyone, to jump the line, jump someone and get ahead. To corrupt someone. The things I put this woman through are objectionable, revolting. I poison my way forward, but I know I am brave, I am being primed for a destiny, for a revolution—I am a leader, all leaders go through the hero's journey, and this is mine, a call to action, adventure. There is only one other man known in history to have drunk kerosene and come out alive. Until he dies, of course—it's a deadly substance, for goodness' sake, and there can only be one brave person alive in the world: me. I am a thrill-seeker, a seeker of unique nature, an asylum seeker.

I get back home from the hospital, the bottle of kerosene is gone, and I never see a bottle of Sprite anywhere in the house again. Now, kerosene and gasoline trigger a memory in me, I always want a Sprite when I see a gas truck drive by. A gas station kiosk with Sprite is heaven.

Trouble befalls all of us. I am not the only pain-in-the-ass child my mother must deal with. Angel is as reckless as me sometimes, and to my mother, and all caring mothers, I should hope, trouble looks the same. I remember Angel standing one afternoon with her mouth wide-open, the sun shining through her teeth like a bright light beaming, as if in an Edward Hopper painting. Right before something dreadful happens to her beautiful teeth.

While she is playing with her friends, a horse-carriage-sized wheelbarrow carrying water drums hits her in the mouth, resulting in her teeth being knocked out. She looks like a cocaine addict—I am talking no visible front teeth. All gone. Angel bursts into tears and news travels fast as she screams. Angel emits loud sounds—rage and pain—but they sound weird because of her no-teeth situation. My mother rushes forward to the front of the house, through the corridor alley of the compound, to the front where my little sister is on the ground crying with her mouth covered in blood. I watch my mother rush to her aid, lifting Angel and placing her on one hip, legs tucked around her. My mother is calm for a bit, as she rocks her back and forth, Angel's head resting on her bosom, then she chases the carrier who flees the scene at a faster rate than any mother carrying a child could match.

To one side of my mother are the neighbours who have been sitting idle watching while kids who have been playing stop and gather around us, making a scene. Angel is in tears and blood. I run inside to grab a towel and bring it to my mother, who puts it around my sister's mouth to stop the bleeding. We come from a spirit of 'it takes a village to raise a child' and today, at this moment, these women, this neighbourhood, this village, failed us, failed my mother. She wants to run to them, but Angel weighs on her, so instead she approaches the ladies cautiously and deadly as they lounge lazily on the cement floor eating crunchy nuts and trading gossip. My mother spares no words. She calls them out for being uselessly idle in a saliva-spitting verbal rhythmic curse. I watch her go from terrified to terrifying instantaneously. Words come out; each word accompanied by a step forward. Word plus action. I sense danger, but she holds back mercifully—Angel can be the only one seen crying, and she needs help. Still, she will have the last word, spat with saliva like a performer in the zone in a heightened scene. With that last curse, she turns around and takes Angel to a hospital where they treat her.

Angel will be okay, and we have risen to the challenge again. Courageous and tremendous are what we will be known as in history. But it's not enough, we need another cautionary tale, so the week after this incident the gods arrange another test of our resilience. This time, while playing in the house,

Angel gets an orange seed stuck in her nose. I don't know if a seed stuck up a nostril can stop breathing long enough to kill someone, but my mother believes this to be the case and once again we rise to the occasion. I run down the street to a bus stop and hail the bus driver, while behind me my mother carries Angel in a front-backpack style, like a tourist in Angola protecting their valuables.

With all that jiggling up and down the street, in one anticlimactic moment a single orange seed comes flying out of Angel's nostril, through the air to the ground. Suddenly, the scene is dull. The comedic rush unwarranted. We all turn around and start walking back home.

All these accidents happen while my father is at work. My mother is our core parent, while my father works on a way to get us out of here and beyond. He works and works and works, determined to break a general generational curse, but things don't seem to get better for us. Nothing holds. Our existence is a filtration bucket of water, full of holes at the bottom.

My mother prepares me for what's coming, an uncertain future, right or wrong. She has a knack for it, handling uncertainty. Her calm presence is out of this world. Every other asylum seeker is desperate and panicking, but she has admirable firm belief. She places her faith in supernatural phenomena and prophetic preachers. I have yet to see her truly freak out. It will terrify me when this happens, but it's inevitable—the rage, angst and depression that lead to the imploding and exploding of every single atom one holds dear as part of 'self'.

We are in limbo here in Dar es Salaam. The only thing I can think of that is keeping us on track is our desire and hope for a better future. A longing for a better outside. My mother has the most hope in our house. It brings her comfort, nourishes her soul. At this point in our journey, the longing is written all over my mother's face.

A few months have gone by since we arrived in Tanzania, and my mother is folding clothes in the bedroom while I play with my toys on the floor. Outside, bullets are being traded among locals. Ammunition is the coloniser's greatest cancer cell in almost all African nations. Inflict and dispense—watch things fall apart.

I am raised with hope, but it doesn't rub off on me. For me, the hardest thing about being in Tanzania is the lies. My parents tell me and Angel that we shouldn't tell anyone where we are from, in a kind of 'it might come back to bite us' way. We are Hutu because my father is Hutu. And Hutus are being chased and killed now. I must keep my friends at arm's length, keep my mouth shut. They will catch us if I slip up. If any of us slip up and tell the truth. The UNHCR will ask my father, 'Why are you working?' and he will not have a truthful answer for them. They will ask how he got a work permit. They will ask if the Tanzanian government acknowledges our asylum and, if so, they will process our resettlement case, not Malawi. But everyone knows now that Malawi is better for refugees needing resettlement. It's a new sanctuary. Camps get old, apparently. Its newness and small size allow more incoming refugees, and people are travelling from Kenyan camps to Malawi. The more numbers come, the more quickly the UNHCR helps everyone to get out. Resettlement. The politics of people.

I want to stay here, keep my sanity—my transparent colour. I don't want to be labelled a refugee, to be tainted, my future detained; to be given shame by the word 'refugee', as if I am sub-human or something, as if I have failed at life.

I am a child—how can I fail? I just started. I want to walk into a room and not have a translator speak for me— Chinese whispers or horse whispers, no, no more. I'll speak up! I don't want to go knocking on countries' doors to accept me and my family, to give us shelter. I have a home. I cannot fight for it—I am too young to—but it's mine. And so close to me while I am still here in Africa. Once help arrives, it will put further distance between me and Cyangugu, Rwanda.

My mother has left all her sisters behind in Rwanda. She misses celebrations with them, weddings, birthdays, everything in between and beyond—they are all she has left since her brother died. It's building up, the fear, crippling, so near—so very clear—implosion. She is doing it again, folding clothes, and I watch her do it. I watch her be somewhere else while doing a mundane task, routinely. She has become too good at this. Folding clothes—mine, Angel's, my father's—on autopilot, mastering domestic chores, using the time for something else, channelled into an otherworldly dreamland. Places of contemplation. Hope of seeing her siblings again. One activity after another. From cleaning dishes to sweeping. Putting Angel and me to bed. It is all well thought out—repeating tasks, consistently jumping from one thought to the next, religiously planning a route out of here.

Being here is a high-wire act of the highest stakes; to seek asylum is a dare. Truth or dare? We are too close to Rwanda, and we need to go further away. Further than exiles can go. Threats will follow us. We need a ticket out of here, fuck the process of resettlement. I need to be on the next rocket now, family-size. I wipe my tears, swipe my fears—will I ever come back again to this place, come back home? Will I ever see these people again, see Musa again?

My father, Seba, has a plan from a friend. The friend is going to guide us, like a sherpa, out of the outskirts of Tanzania and all the way to Dzaleka, Malawi, for registration. Soon we will pack and leave, take a bus via Karonga, north Malawi—past Lake Malawi into the middle of the country, making a stop at Karonga refugee camp. It is a transit refugee camp, and we stay there briefly, awaiting our verdict.

The results come in and we move further. My father carries Angel. My mother carries me on the way, and if you have had the pleasure of previewing my childhood photos, you will know this is a heavy-duty task. Eventually and finally, we arrive in Dzaleka refugee camp. At first it is a relief for my mother to put my chubby body down in Dzaleka, but then another feeling floods through her, floods through all of us: grief. It will be many years before home is within reach again. Malawi will be our exile for the next fourteen years. We will be stranded here, temporal beings. Our exit is unknown and not within our control at all—we are doomed to a life of trying, going up against luck with as much grace as possible.

Upon arrival all new refugees must register who they are and their residency so they can receive food stamps and get supplies from the World Food Program. My father registers me, despite my reluctance, because I am better than this. My mother and my sister play along: suckers. And just like that, Seba has a refugee status of the year 2000, stamped and everything.

Departing Dar es Salaam, the goodbye to Musa is looming. He is my first real friend. I will miss his kindness, humour and, most of all, his adventurous spirit. He is fearless, always up for trouble, and I love him. His mother and father are talking—gossiping, in fact, whispering about our departure.

By the time he confronts me, he knows already deep down that I am going. I won't be able to give him my new number or new address. I spend the night with him watching films, pretending we will always do this. When the bus arrives outside our compound, Musa and I share our goodbyes.

I can't quite remember his face now, his features. I am holding on to this story, to every line like a vein, a contour of his face, the borders that will soon be my only memory and point of connection to Musa—and Tanzania.

I honestly remember little of my time in Tanzania. Maybe I am being selective. Oh Lord, help me. Deliver me from this dementia, amnesia—cultural and political. I don't want it; I want to remember. I want my childhood back. I want my future right.

No one feels sorry for me or my family when we arrive in Dzaleka. Empathy is a bourgeoisie class privilege. We are all in the same horrible situation here. In an impossible predicament. Not knowing what happens next. My mother is supportive through my implosion, taking the mother's role in its best sense. My mother prays and I play. My mother is serious, and I am silly. My mother is hoping, and I am hopping. Both requiring a leap of faith and a quantum belief.

Many camps have been built to accommodate refugees fleeing Congo, Burundi and Rwanda. So many of us are thrust into the storm of being on the run, homesick. Of wanting to go back, but being unable to—then how far into the future can you go? Holding out a torch for the best nations the world offers, yelling, 'Pick me! Pick me! I promise you, what I feel is real.'

My primary concern being here is how much I miss Musa. I keep thinking he is coming to visit, and glancing at my parents' faces, thinking, 'He is coming to see me at some point, right?' If I had asked my parents, they would probably have asked me, 'Do you think Auntie Shema is coming to visit us too?' I don't ask. I wonder and slowly stop wondering and make new friends that I will say goodbye to later when I move to Australia.

Here in Dzaleka, we join the local church, as we are devout Christians. Refugees pray a lot, at least my family does. A prayer is a story, being told to an audience of one. A sincere narrative, one that implies both parties know what's going on, an agreement. I love praying. Saying what is obvious, total freedom, nothing to hide, He sees all.

At some point I stop praying though. At some point, I don't know when, I find I can't be a romantic anymore. I stop believing the parables. 'God is testing you' suddenly seems ridiculous. As that old joke goes, 'If God is testing us, I prefer to take a written.' I stop believing in God, but I never stop believing in parables, in stories. I have the urge to tell a story myself, narrate my journey. Relay the message. Keep my lineage—who I am.

Storytelling is a part of daily life here in the camp, too. There is a story going around that there has only been one power outage in US history—it went on for a whole day, and everyone who worked on this unfortunate day was fired. The story is told and retold around bonfires and in huts with no electricity. People dreaming. Projecting. Wishing to place themselves in the pre-brutal moments of that day.

This story, of course, is not true, but serves a delicious purpose of hope. Here in Malawi, power outages are frequent. In such instances, candlelight illuminates our houses, our paths, and ability to see forward, to see a future. Lo and behold.

II

IN DZALEKA REFUGEE CAMP, MY father opens a mini store with money he scraped together. The kind you still might find in Australian suburbia, where the kiosk connects to the house. I'm that little kid doing homework while selling you phone credit.

Dzaleka refugee camp is intense, but having been thrown into its arms we are relieved finally to be here. It's a hard place to describe. Many people have not experienced what it's like to be in a refugee camp, to be a refugee, a vagabond, a hoodlum. It is a harrowing place. We have nothing in common, all of us gathered here, except that we want to go to some other place. We are waiting for governments to choose our new homes. I feel dumb. This feels dumb, numb and hopeless. There are thousands of us. The only other place I can think of that accumulates thousands of people who have nothing to do is a prison. But this is not a prison. It cannot be, surely. Are we being punished?

Malawi is struggling with its own problems, and they hate refugees being here. They call the civil unrest that brought us here the wind of destruction, the wiping out of a million plus people in my home country of Rwanda, a purifying massacre. We are cockroaches, they say, infidels— ethnic cleansing was needed. We are hooligans, blood-sucking vampires. We are occupying space and taking away opportunities that should go to the pure ones. If this is how a home country feels about extending a helping hand to us, of familiar languages and principles, what is to become of us then, here in exile?

I doubt NGOs have any clue what is really going on in camps—the food scarcity, dirty water, widespread diseases. I am too young to understand how this creates a narrow path for me and my family. Not much is expected of the disenfranchised. Here in Dzaleka, I am stuck. We are stuck, all of us. Rwandese, Congolese, Burundians, Ugandans. We are in limbo—a liminal space—in the refugee camp. The cries of those left behind are, 'Come home. It's safe now, just come home. We want you home.'

I look at a family photo we have in which I am being held up close. Close to the neck of Caliste, my grandfather, my father's father. You cannot tell it's me. The photo looks bad, blurry. The shutter speed must have not been right for the day or maybe it was taken before they started using acetate in film, a safer, more accurate sheet. I want this image preserved. My teeth in the photo are visible shining through the lens. You can see my smile. Caliste has a blue suit on, his eyes pensive. The red brick layered house we stand in front of is the house my father grew up in. Costasie, my father's mother, is not in the photo, but she is the one who is still alive. Women outlive men where I am from.

Why can't we go back home and see my grandmother? Before it's too late, before it costs too much to fly home. The telegram says it's safe now. My father will say nothing about it. He assumes I don't know, and that I don't see his face, the one that says, 'My hands are not so much tied as they are empty.' He has nothing to show for his return.

The red-brick-layered house from the photo has been put up for sale by my father's siblings. And he is not there for the bidding war. All wars are bid on. It's a sick game. He is fighting for it. To keep it, to hold the memories. The goal, for him and my mother is to move back one day—to live there. They are moving on, everyone who survived. They must, too much has been lost to swim in that pool of 'what is lost, who is gone'.

It is important to keep a barometer for your hopes. If you find yourself in a temporary escape of an atrocious vagabond pit-hole, such as me and my family here, do not, and I repeat, do not get your hopes up at all. And slowly you will learn, as we did, that here in limbo you must move time forward. Fast enough to arrive at the promised land.

My family is coasting off a friend of my father's generous welcoming. Baba Angelo is a great friend of my father.

He takes us in when we first arrive in Dzaleka, and we stay with him. The hospitality and grace of my father's friend are wonderful, but we must chip in. We have to sweep and mop the cement floors, clean the house. We must also help by fetching water. Mpopi is Chichewa for faucet. The number of faucets in the camp are about three or four. They are placed in locations at the centre of the maze— the central town area. Everyone can access them from their radius. I know where all of them are located. I know that the closest one to Baba Angelo's house is always busy with mothers that cut the line because, well, they have priority— kids to take to school early in the morning and so on. The alternative is to wake up at 4 am to better my chances, but that's not happening because I love my sleep.

If we're not in line for food or water, we're in line for something else, so I perfect a trick to cut lines for the days I need to collect food from the World Food Program. These lines are long. Not only do refugees in the camp come to collect food, but also those who have settled outside Dzaleka, who maintain a false residency in the camp. This results in constant food shortage, so line jumping is good. I should give a disclaimer that this trick I am about to reveal has a short life span once it's out there.

My sister Angel and I line up for food but never next to each other because this will, in fact, ruin the trick. I hold the food-stamp ticket and she stands in line without one, and as we get close to the truck—it must be very close to the truck to make the trick worthwhile—she will fake a faint, full-blown theatrics. Her bucket drops first and then her legs stop moving and then her whole body follows. To the floor. Good-hearted people gather around in a circle, leaving my sister to be a griot, a jali, in the middle, surrounded by narratives, a queen picking threads of stories to tell an audience. Their hands are on their mouths gasping while they panic, giving each other looks of 'who could help this little girl?', 'who here is a doctor?', knowing none of us are. As a moving silhouette of me passes by, Angel's eyes come back to consciousness, in time to give a look. 'Go on, brother, go on,' the look says. 'I will keep distracting them, go all the way to the front.' As soon as I advance up the line, she comes back to life, one bone after another, like a robot booted up.

My youngest sister Boni is born and is diagnosed with Down syndrome soon after our arrival. She needs a specialist to see regularly, a miracle worker. The camp only provides basic medical needs. We need a physiotherapist from the city, but it would not work financially to commute into the city for her much-needed hospital visits. UNHCR in Dzaleka gives us a permit—an exit out, and into Lilongwe, temporarily. We may live there, as opposed to Dowa, where Dzaleka is. We pack up, moving the kiosk and the house to Lilongwe, the capital city of Malawi.

Summer in Malawi is stunning. It's around harvest season and everything we planted the year before is ripe and ready. Across from my house there is an enormous mulberry tree. It's massive, taking me and three friends to wrap around it. I love mulberries because they are twice as long as blackberries and bigger; it's twice the sweetness and the joy, yum! In Malawi we call mulberries 'mabulosi'.

This summer, mabulosi are bigger and blacker with a tinge of red from the sun hitting them directly from above. My friend Sautso stands waiting to go next. I grab my white plastic bag to keep all mabulosi in. I take off my slippers. I tie my white plastic bag on my belt loop. I am hands-free and ready to climb.

As I am progressing branch after branch of the tree, Sautso is screaming, 'To your left, Oli! No, to the right! Yes, a couple of big ripe ones! Right there.' I see them, pluck some and throw them in my bag. The bag is almost full now. From the bottom, the view is better. Sautso keeps pointing towards the blacker berries. From Sautso's view you can already see the fruits of my labour. The red juice from ripe berries crushing at the bottom of my white plastic bag. A few more picks and I launch my descent.

I get to the bottom with all my berries. I untie the bag. It's 4 pm at this point and the sun is setting. Mother calls me. It's dinnertime. I share some mabulosi with Sautso and say goodbye. I put on my slippers and start rushing home.

Running back home, I see my father's 1988 cream hard-body Nissan pickup truck pulling over. The tinted windows are up, but I can still hear Rwandan gospel playing loudly. With tinted windows and loud gospel music, my father seems like a God-fearing drug dealer. In the back of the truck is a crate of drinks he has bought. I help him bring the drinks inside the house. He is home early today because it is Christmas, a special time for the family.

Earlier today, we were at church like every year on Christmas Day. We are Pentecostal, so the passionate praise of the one and only Lord in heaven is always turned to maximum during Christmas. Every year we put on the nativity play. I have my reservations about this play. I feel it's missing something. Missing me. They have not cast me again this year. I am salty about that, yes. I can play one of the innkeepers. The one that says, 'No room for the saviour of the world in here, move along.' Or I can play the person who holds the star that the three wise men follow. Surely that's easy, no lines, just tracking. Even Sautso got a part playing one of the wise men. It's ironic because Sautso is an idiot. After the play, the singing, and the praises. We go home for dinner.

At the dinner table, only my father is sitting on a chair. Not because he is the king and no one else is allowed; he sits there alone because of how small the table is. It's less a table and more a dinner stool. My sisters and I are sitting down on a floor mat. T. B. Joshua is on TV. My mother has finished making beef stew in the kitchen, I know this because humming tunes have stopped. She says humming is the secret ingredient to good food. We say grace and we eat. After a deliciously filling dinner, bottles of Fanta and Coca-Cola, it's bedtime. Another good Christmas.

At 4 in the morning, I hear these voices, loud voices. And they're getting louder and louder. Too close, too real. Something is about to happen. What is happening? I am eleven years old. My memories are blurry. Tainted, grey even. I remember waking up to two rifles pointing at me. Pointing at me to command my surrender. The rifles are aimed at their target—me—so precisely that if they fire, they will not miss. I can look down the barrel of my decider. Life and death staring directly at me. Their fingers are on the triggers.

'Iwe! Iwe!' they scream at me, waking me from my dreamlike state. 'Tenga zovala zako, munyamuke lero kutipa kwanu!' Which, in a nutshell, translates to 'Get the fuck out of here.'

I hear what he is saying to me, but my body cannot move. 'Iwe, Iwe!' they scream again.

My parents are in the other room with the commanding officer, who asks, 'Anakuza ndandi kuti mukhale kuno?'

My mind is racing and tracing for crumbs of hope in the soldiers' eyes, but—fuck—I cannot make eye contact with men of power, I am raised better. I am scared with every utterance of words, in Chichewa. You made me learn this language and now you don't want me here. Oh, Lord.

The commanding officer asks my father another question: 'Ndiwe othawa kwawo?'

'Eya,' Father says.

'Chifukwa chani ulikuno m'malo mwa Dzaleka?'

Father responds, 'Ndilindi chilolezo.' He reaches into a drawer next to his bed. He grabs a permit that confirms everything he has been communicating with the commanding officer, who snatches the document, has a good look at it before giving it back.

I am facing down, my fingers crossed. With as much courage left in me, I un-bow my head and stare into the gun barrel and meet my maker. Suddenly, given we have the legitimate permit, the commanding officer rounds up all the soldiers to leave. The two soldiers in my room slowly back away and I see the gap opening. Only now do I slowly breathe again, like a recently submerged free diver coming up for air.

The entire ordeal took about thirty minutes, but it felt like forever.

My mother comes to my room. At the sight of her, I calm down. 'Go back to bed, Oli,' she says. Mother then goes to the other room and puts my sisters to bed. I lie awake in my bed, wallowing in the shame, feeling unwanted.

I go to work with my father to help out with the kiosk restocking. I wake up at 3 or 4 am, depending on the amount of labour to be carried out. The trips we make to the countryside sometimes take hours, half a day. A head start is needed if we are to get there in time before the farmers have brought out their fresh harvest (corn, nuts, beans) for my father to buy so we can sell it later in the kiosk.

The drive is long, and I catch up on my rest, having been woken up at an hour that night guards finish their shifts. I am deep dozing in the passenger seat. Whip, my father's car, the Nissan, wobbles. It goes over a ditch, bouncing up and down. Natural speed bumps. I am on a racetrack road. With every turn, it feels like the whole thing is going to come apart. He is not a skilled driver, my father, not like I am. But he is sufficient—a cabbie requirement—we are alive. He and the road have a pact to not let me recover my ultradian naps. I bounce off the dusty car seat, giving him a side-eye but not saying anything.

I love taking these trips as I get to spend time with my father. I rarely see him. I mean, as a father. I see him in my school fees and clothes and food, but as a figure to hang out with, not really. We are not close, and whose fault is that? His. I am perfect. I am a child. I never make mistakes. I am a diamond made of pressure. Diamonds are the hardest mineral on earth, only a diamond can cut into another diamond. I am impenetrable, he cannot cut me, because he is not made of diamonds. I will take all he throws at me and come out stronger. I am a child, his child.

When we arrive, I lay down a tent, which has been stolen from UNHCR in Dzaleka, and dust rises tornado style. The sun hitting the massive tent dries the harvests. Farmers flock to us like bees to honey. I set up a pyramid using sticks and use the tip knot to hang our scale loose. Business is going down. Labour, labour of love. Wet harvests are not good for business: no one wants to buy them—plus it makes the harvest heavier than it is on the scale, a cheat code farmers used to get more cash out of us. They don't fool me anymore. I have been foolish before, my father made a note of it and added beatings to my tab of scolding.

On this wonderful bright morning I am kneeling at the far edge of the tent, where UNHCR is printed in sky blue, spreading nuts. I look over my shoulder at my father and see how focused he is, and I think about what drives a man to train a child, his son (myself), to manoeuvre through the world in this arena of business (toughness). He doesn't see it how I see it, a bonding one-on-one time. He is training me, preparing me.

At the end of the day our tent is full, heavy, bearing the weight of harvest we just bought. Today was good at the markets. A good gravity day. The tent dips in the middle, its submission a sign of our success. But it also means I won't be coming back here for a while, until we run out. This means less time spent with my father.

I stay awake on the drive home even though I am tired. Driving away from villages and farms, wind blows in my face, I keep an eye out. The ride back is less bumpy because of the heavy load of harvest in the back of the pickup truck. We get to our home in Chinsapo, Lilongwe. Our house is attached to the duka—kiosk—and I unload the goods and get them inside. It's a heavy load that will aggravate my father's back problems. He goes straight inside for dinner, leaving me to offload everything.

At dinner:

'Ba—tell me about where I am from? What was my grandfather like?'

'When you are all grown up, I will.'

'But I am now.'

'Ah, I mean when you are not an idiot.'

'Ija chakuja chako. Okay.' Eat your meal.

The red-brick-layered apartments that surround Hawa's place are bright, and yet dark, burgundy almost. I know how these bricks are made. I know how to make them—I have done it many times as an early teenager. I am a jack of all trades. You can be one too. Just pick a war, any war, and get on the wrong side of it, then spend years seeking asylum, safety, years of accumulating skills to survive. I guarantee that one of those skills is going to be how to build a house, a home, brick by brick.

A good brick takes a while to put together. Dirty water is mixed with mud or soil, formulating the brick solution. It must be dirty, the water. Back home, clean water is preserved for something else—someone else. You mix soil with dirty water, and it always makes solid bricks. Solid foundation too. The process, which takes days, starts as follows. A strong shirtless boy such as me digs a ditch for keeping the mix—the type of ditch serial murder-mystery documentaries features. Another man, a carpenter normally, crafts a timber brick model to shovel the mixture in. The strong youthful man then chucks in the mix and flips the model on the ground for the sun to dry the bricks (only a fool makes bricks in the rainy season, and there is always one fool in town). One brick at a time.

Making them red is separate. It requires patience. And lots of fire. Inferno. First things first. The strong youth and another person lay and stack bricks one by one, Jenga-style, till we have a massive square chunk the size of a small Toyota bus. We add all the while, leaving a tunnel at the bottom (a hollow space for fire), or several, depending on the size of oven and the number of bricks. At this stage, the bricks have been baking in the sun for about two to four weeks. They are solid and ready to go to a place of cooking, the oven. We mix another batch of mud to cover the Jenga of bricks, ensuring the baking—the burning fire—will be as potent as hell itself. Then I gather more timber.

All of this takes place at a location far from people or flammable things. If anything went up in flames, we'd have to wait two days for the slow Malawian fire trucks to get to us. It would be a sluggish unfolding of a disaster. We hand-pick a bare field where the trees have been cut down to become timber for the cooking and baking of the bricks. The timber I have gathered is then ushered into the tunnels and the fire lit. Four weeks have gone by at this stage. We monitor the first ignition of fire, and then we keep checking it and adding more timber. Evening and night come—we trade, watching like guards protecting an

Egyptian kingdom through the night; we add more timber and watch over it through the night. Rinse, repeat.

Smoke smoulders less and less towards the end of the burn and you can always see the fire imprints on brown–black bricks turn red. You look at the small van of an oven and you see red in the cracks; peeling it off, you can see the red bricks layered together. A classic traditional craftsman-ship that preserves our theatres, museums, powerhouses, and apartments.

I can't help but remember this process as I walk into the red apartment complex Hawa lives in. It is my first visit to her place. She lives in Redbank, a predominantly black neighbourhood in Queensland. I am here to tutor her in literary studies. It's been a year and a bit since arriving in Australia. And this is the first job I enjoy. It's definitely not the same as making bricks, but then again, I am a jack of all trades.

Hawa is seventeen and I am almost nineteen. She is about to graduate from secondary school. She is a dark-skinned African-Australian girl, lovely and bright. Our first sessions we go through some stories. I am about to get into university so I can get my writing degree. This is my side hustle that will help me earn pocket money while I study. Hawa is from Tanzania, though she doesn't tell me this. Not yet anyway. She only lets me see what she wants me to see. Which at this stage is what's inside this nice red-brick-layered apartment. Inside, it's warm and I take off my shoes when I go in. She doesn't ask, but at some places you just know. The almost cashmere rug meets my socks and I experience ultimate comfort. I want to rub my face in it. I go over to the couch. The TV is not on, kids don't live in this place. It's toy-free and clean, like a model designer house, one that's always empty, occupied only by inspiration. The transparent work desk where we're set up is neat. It's one of those one-leg-only perfectly balanced architecture desks, minimal. Hawa's apartment is owned by white people. I mean, like, her foster parents are white. I remember thinking, this all makes sense now, after seeing them.

Hawa is not adopted. She lives here because her African parents kicked her out of the house. And I relate. She has one of those big families and they feud a lot. About this and the other. The other this time resulting in her leaving home earlier than she intended. We bond, me and Hawa, about our dysfunctional family stories. My parents have at various points kicked me out of home, left me on the kerb and pavement. Her family lives in another part of Redbank. She sees them from time to time. We are making significant progress in our tutoring sessions. We become more acquainted, and she tells me all about Tanzania. We laugh about home stories. I love hearing her talk more about it— home, her home. My home as well, once.

In the early 2010s, a truck appears at the front porch of our house and kiosk. A Toyota Dyna truck. I am so excited about it. I will inherit this car, of course. It is shiny, glorious even. Pure white, like Jesus' white robe. A clean and new one, recently manufactured for sure. If I ever saw my father love any object, it's this car. It puts a smile on his face, a genuine smile on his face. So, when I reverse crush it into a wall a few months later, he is furious to say the least.

The victim wall is the garage nearby where we keep the truck. My father has relied on the garage to protect his car since the radio and battery got stolen from the Nissan (RIP) two months ago when it was parked in our backyard. If the thieves had had time, they would probably have stolen the tyres and engine too, quite common in these parts of Malawi. I see three things on his face when I break the news of having hit a wall with his truck to him. Shame, disappointment and anger. It's not my fault though. He is supposed to teach me to drive, but every time he lets me drive, I am sitting in the passenger seat steering for only a minute before he takes back control of the car.

When I hit the garage wall, I step on the brake and the owner comes rushing out screaming, 'Go forward!' I panic and freeze. 'Out,' he says. 'Out,' he yells again. I drive out of the garage and then back home to hand my father the keys and give him the news. He goes back to the garage, parks the car properly and apologises on my behalf to the owner. I expect a beating which doesn't come. Is he retiring? Tiring? But then I think he feels what I feel. Shame.

I'm a teenager, fifteen years old, maybe, when I return home from going out with friends and I am scolded by my parents for no reason. 'Ukufuta chamba ndi gulu lako,' they say. You were smoking weed with the gang again. It's a chorus repeating in my eardrums. I haven't yet, but they believe otherwise. Also, gangs are hard to find in Malawi. I truly wish I could get recruited. If I could get inside a gang, we would have exciting stories to trade. Me and my gang would be true rebels—spend most of our childhood in and out of jail. Because of small-time robberies, they will give us our gang names in jail: GOBALILOS and Vikes and Malawi's Most Notable Baddest Bois (MMNBB). We will settle for GOBALILOS. In jail with my gang, of which I will be the leader, I will have selected trusted members only, recruiting newcomers once every five years. Only niggas serving at least a ten-year sentence have a chance. We will have the longest reign. They will try to convert us to Islam, but we will rebel and read Baldwin, Fanon and pre-jail Mandela. Become notorious, radicalised, break out of jail and launch the most perfectly planned and executed political coup. No one will die and there will be a documentary in which my parents—in exile since I took over the country—emotionally tell the reporters and documentary people how they suspected something when I came home smelling of cannabis. This is how it will go down, but for now I settle for their shouting and cautionary tales. Tales of wasting my future. They say this is the reason they don't share family stories with me.

My father is supposedly a family man, but I do not find him particularly expressive of anything except anger or indifference. He is a man of few words. A list of his favourite words: family, church, Jesus, God and heaven. Father's specialty is to beat now and ask later. Imagine an after-pay beating service—an after-ask service. There is no reasonable doubt. He beats me when I don't speak up about my reason for being out late. I am left with two choices anyone has in my position: cry or speak. I take the beating. I get used to them. Tears roll down my cheeks and I taste my salt. There is a distance growing between my father and me, stitching up my mouth deeper. As I get older, he stops beating me. I can't remember when, but in my mind, there is a before and after period. Before respect, care, parenting or joy. But in case I get complacent with my newfound peace, he reminds me, 'Just because I am old, don't think that you can take me.' A real fighter's spirit runs through his veins.

Right now, on this late night, before his retirement, I take the beating, and my younger sisters take a masterclass out of this as always. I hate being the first. The one everyone learns from, learning ways to not piss off our father.

I sob in my bed, which is in the living room. A mattress on the floor. Even this I can't experience in private. Humiliation descends on me. The perk of being poor is unglamorous grief, so I sob in the living room sitting on my bed. I wait for everyone to finish watching TV to sleep.

Before I sleep, I kneel and pray, not for my father's demise, though I have thought about it many times. I pray to not wet my bed. I am a massive bedwetter well into my teens—which makes it a difficult time for a younger me. I do not know whether in the morning I'll be swimming in my own tears or piss. Plus, bedwetting would be added to my tab of beatings. Through all of this, I forget about my curiosity about my family. What was a genuine curiosity of mine is now a teenager's fantasy of how I will get away with murder, the murder of my father. I can take Seba, I think to myself, not really believing it. On my return from parkour afternoon sessions with the gang, I think I can backflip on him. But parkour is a recoiling skill, useless in an actual fight. My best tactic is a somersault on my father. If I can land it.

III

At 4 am, I hear noises outside our small place. My time has come, I know it. Honestly, the noises are calling me. I hear chanting noises. I am terrified. The voices get louder, screaming, 'Mfiti! Mfiti!' I realise a crime has been committed; the voices are protesting now, and not white people protesting, which almost always involves a picnic at the end, this one involves angry black people—it will probably lead to a riot. They are using the most powerful tool a mob has—piles of bricks, stones. 'Mfiti!'—witch— they scream and scream. Taking the role of a wake-up call, normally reserved for roosters.

By the time I hear the chanting, the whole neighbourhood has surrounded a nearby house with torches as if it's the seventeenth century, they are ready to burn a witch to ashes. This is not unheard of in Malawi. They do burn witches. At that moment, I think to myself, I hope I am not a witch one of these days, then another thought comes just as quickly, but I would make a great one. They would never catch me. All my footprints and footnotes would be legendary tales only comparable to Chinua Achebe. Grand heroic stories. I am formidable—a savage, bow before me.

I would love to dispute some people's thoughts about African voodoo, but a lot of it is true. People do spiritual and superstitious acts for the most of basic wishes: food on the table, the neighbour's house to catch fire. They visit witch doctors.

There is a ranking for seeking help in poor countries. It goes from bottom to top: pastor, sheikh, monk, doctor, police, shaman, rabbi, fortune-teller, magician—and then a witch doctor (all-encompassing and very cheap too). Magicians and witch doctors have one thing in common: secrets. One of them is more noble. I won't say which one, but you know. A witch doctor is going to make your stomach pain go away, your jealous neighbour respect you more. They will not solve a murder for you. That would be nice if they could. But alas, not in this lifetime.

When I walk past the witch doctors in Lilongwe, I avoid eye contact with them (you don't want to make them angry) while simultaneously trying to see their carpet of potions. They seem to have everything: a jar full of bird bones, a doll resembling one's aunt on each side of the family, odd cloth, meat balls. One girl tells me she used a potion of juju as a love spell to win a man's heart. It involved period blood and chamomile tea. To which my question was, 'Whose blood was it? Yours?' as if it would make a difference.

Voodoo of any kind is not taken lightly in parts of Africa. If you ever see an African witch burning, then you will know. If you have not witnessed one of these, I highly recommend it, but I would recommend starting off easy. Go to Nollywood and watch some out-there voodoo films to get you prepped for the actual burning, as it can be intense. *Burial of Kojo* is a personal favourite of mine. Then you can book your ticket to a secluded village in west Africa, Mali maybe, and start your journey—best of luck!

This morning they are gathered outside my friend Donald's house, a chubby boy I have met through soccer. Donald talks way too much. He is also an easy target for his father's beatings. We have that in common. Otherwise, I do not know why we are friends. He is lazy and a liar. He also has a habit of stealing. He goes around the area, stealing what people hang on their clothing lines. Shoes, jackets, panties, socks, kitchen clothes, curtains—all magically find their way into his closet, neatly folded like a star boy. I want to get a witch doctor to curse him, send him bad omens, make his fat toes even fatter. I am not jealous of his fresh stolen stuff. Well, maybe a little. But mainly because he stole my shoes and denied it while wearing them. The balls on this fat nigga.

I will not have to resort to going to a witch doctor and possibly curse Donald, because it turns out the universe has already done that. Donald leaves his house at 4 am and quickly wishes he hadn't.

Before I tell you the full story, let me share with you the reason Donald is outside the house at this hour. You ask anyone who grew up very poor in parts of Africa and they will tell you that there is but one reason our protagonist, this fat conniving thief, is heading out of a house straight after he wakes—he needs to take a shit. An act I think should be exempt for poor people, by the way, given how infrequently food falls into their lap. Someone should talk to the authorities about that—not me, obviously, I have adventures to experience, stories to live through and tell later. Toilets in most parts of Africa are built outhouse style, a hole in the ground to be specific. It can be gross. I have seen toilets too close to a water well and I am, like, they will meet at some point—that's not safe or hygienic. Sometimes the outhouses are communal with multiple holes in the ground. I have heard stories of people falling into a well of shit because the concrete has given up holding weight. It's risky business.

At about 4 am, Donald feels the need to take a shit after what I presume was a good but gassy evening meal hours and hours before. Potatoes with beans, alongside nsima perhaps. Nsima + therere, mbewa + ugali, nyemba + mpunga are among the various food combinations that cause shit-taking in the morning. Donald wakes up in his bed. On the walls of his room are posters of people he will never meet or get any closer to. David Beckham is one. If these walls could talk. He lights a candle to carry and walks out into the corridor of the house, another risky business. Then it's a straight walk for a couple of metres until he's outside. He is barefoot and hopes it will be a quick dump and back to sleep.

Outside his house is a backyard. Enough for a party of ten. But this morning, it's a party for one. One wicked witch. Most villagers here, superstitious or not, will sprinkle magic powder around the house. They buy it from witch doctors to protect themselves from witches or, if you are my mother, then you sprinkle holy water. All to avoid this very moment Donald is about to go through.

It's a 500-metre walk to the toilet, but as soon as he takes two steps from the back door of his house, he knows what he has stepped into. A pile of shit. Not just any shit. A wicked witch's shit. That's what witches typically do. They run and shit at someone's house, at least here in Malawi—I am sure in Vermont it's different. The house right now, it's Donald's. I am telling this story as I heard it. What happens next is that Donald screams at exactly the time the witch comes back for another lap.

Oh, please pick a war, any war. And then you can live the way I live and experience this. One day, you will tell stories like this.

The witch locks eyes with Donald and she screams. I know, right, you would think witches would be exempt from emotions of any kind. Anyway, then Donald screams some more, freaked out at the sight of a naked old lady. Yes, naked. The witch recoils from the light of Donald's candle, mortified. But Donald can only see sections of the witch illuminated by the candle, and in the shadowy shapes the shadows create, he imagines more witches around the house. He freaks out some more and goes into a frenzy, screaming and kicking shit. The wicked witch retreats to the toilet, screaming, and Donald runs into the house.

Everyone in the house is awake now, and more lanterns are lit. Donald's mother and little brother get up and try to rush outside, but Donald stops them at the door and points to the shit on the ground and all over him now. Then he points to the toilet. Frantically, he tells them what's happened. Donald's father tiptoes around the landmine (shit), slowly making his way towards the toilet. Inside, he finds a curled-up, shivering witch. And something magical happens. There is a recognition moment between the two strangers, which shatters the mystery glass altogether. She is the beer brewer from next door, their neighbour.

Donald's father lifts her off the floor and tries to help her home. It's 5 am at this point and the noise has woken up a few people. They are spooked by the sight of a naked lady being escorted out of a toilet. They scream, 'Mfiti, Mfiti.' By the time Donald and his father get her inside her place, a crowd has formed outside.

People gather next to a pile of stones. It is an old-school style of punishment—stoning this witch to death. Elders of the village demand a civil discourse and try to lead a negotiation process diplomatically. They want to resolve this and find an amicable solution, but the jury continues to discuss the verdict. People are furious. 'This is bullshit,' one person screams. And another goes, 'We do not negotiate with witches!' This one stirs the crowd. 'Yes, bring the witch out!' they cry. It's a cacophony of chaos. Meanwhile, rumours continue to spread and apparently Donald is now the witch, along with his mother, father and brother—they were practising witchcraft and stealing clothing and other things around the neighbourhood. The voodoo is the reason they've gone undetected for months and months. Then another rumour spreads—it's his father who turns into a vampire and goes around the area, practising witchcraft riding a broom. Do vampires ride brooms? Why do they call the witchcraft part of it 'practising'? As if there are non-practising witches, who are just out of the game. Hung up the broomstick and retired.

No one knows what's going on inside, but outside there is now a massive crowd. Three hours have gone by. Food and tea are being consumed while people wait for the wicked witch to be brought outside so they can burn her. Justice served. It's a whole festival, a new wave festival. (Just pick a war, any war.) 'We raise our kids around this witch,' someone yells. Piles of stones resembling the Nubian pyramids lie ready for stoning the lady. Small rocks roll off the top of the house. Anytime now, anytime.

Not much is known about the woman. She has no husband or kids and lives alone. I am scared shitless hearing all these stories. All that is known is that she brews local beer from sorghum and corn grains. Chibuku Shake! Shake! A popular local Malawian brand (you don't shake it twice, though some do—it is just the name of the beer). She sells them at taverns. The alcoholics in the furious crowd congregating outside demand to know what she puts in the beers they buy directly from her. Love potions, I am sure.

This is the last I hear of the wicked witch because the military come and shoot their guns in the sky, dispersing the crowd like scared rats. I never talk to Donald again after that. For all I know he is a witch now or a wizard, which is it? Anyway, the lady's beer-selling licence is taken away, and she moves to another town and continues to experiment with alcoholic beverages.

The story of the witch is told and retold by the community. Societies approach witchcraft differently, whether you are in Connecticut or Chilinde. Or Brisbane. Brisbane's infamous poo jogger should have been deemed a witch in the winter of 2018. But no, when he is caught running and shitting around the neighbourhood in the suburb of Greenslopes, they write it off as a crazy man with an eccentric morning routine. I understand that we all have urges. Some of them cannot be controlled past a certain age, sure. But the poo jogger should have had a crowd outside his front door. I don't know what it is about western countries that they take witchcraft so lightly these days. He gets fined about four hundred Australian dollars and walks away intact. He gets fired from his executive role at a company and thrown back into society. They should take his witchcraft licence away and place him on the non-practising witch list. I have nothing against witches, but 'practising' witches, no.

It is not my fault at all that I end up with her. It is the 2010s, and the singer is everywhere, including Africa, believe it or not. For a long time, I didn't even know she was British. I thought she was just white. I also thought we were losing her to the mob when she almost got cancelled by internet culture vultures for wearing cultural Jamaican things and not being part of it. Then she said, 'But I am dating Skepta.' Everyone backed off after that, but then I thought, isn't he Nigerian? Anyway, you see, back in the mid-nineties when I was just about to be born, men with Kangol hats on around California were investing in boys with flat caps to allow them to come up with innovative tech ideas. The investments and ideas spread through western Europe and northern America—even southern Africa. One of those novel ideas was being fostered by a bald man with a black turtleneck, Steve Jobs. It was that bald man's fault that I ended up with Adele's albums. Apple had promised to change the world and, come the 2000s, one of its promises came to life and made its way to the palms of people's hands—iTunes was here.

Then came the iPod to accommodate the iTunes library. I am ecstatic about the gadget and so is everyone I know in Malawi. The iPod met me at the coming of age and when I had it in my hands for the first time, it felt like nothing in the world could touch me. I was an astronaut with this device in Malawi.

I love anything electronic. I love to open any gadgets, work out what's going on there, waves—radio waves—I must investigate with the help of a Philips. I open every single one that ever crosses my path. No exaggeration. I get into trouble at school for this. I mean, I get in trouble during school, full stop. If I got around to closing the gadgets, I would be square. But I am getting in trouble anyway at school because I am a rebel without a cause, I am breaking a window or not paying school fees or trying unsuccessfully to be a wise arse. I am doing these things all at once while having an energy drink—what a rascal. If I rank the reasons people knock on my mother's door, at the very top would be because I have broken their Walkman or radio. I break televisions and antennas. And, of course, my parents must pay for all these. I break and break. And I do eventually learn how to be good at these things, which is to use them without breaking them, but first a string of bad-luck instances that get me into trouble with my father again.

I brought home a Super Nintendo console one time with an antenna plug. It needs to be connected to a TV antenna port to work and I plug it in to get started. I insert a cartridge from the top of the console to see my games and power it up. Amazingly, it is working. I play games all day until I know my father will close the kiosk and come home. I decide to stop. That's when I break the TV antenna receiver port somehow. I unplug and hide it, hoping to delay what's coming for me. Sometimes I choose to get it out of the way, the beating. If I have things to do, I'll schedule a beating in. Sometimes he'll let it slide altogether and I'll live to fight another day—his retirement is near. And sometimes he doesn't notice I've broken a gadget. But my father's eyes are always glued to that TV box. Only a matter of days, rupture inevitable.

He notices something wrong with the TV a few days later, when I am doing my homework. This is terrible luck and that false hope I built of 'maybe he has forgotten about it all' goes out the window. He didn't notice it for a few days because he was playing gospel-music videos off the DVD player and didn't need the TV channels. I realise this and curse the damn DVD setup. Hope runs its course into oblivion. I get summoned from my bedroom to the living room. And tonight, I will take it again. Another beating with the TV cable (how poetic). He says something like, I must get a new one now. This beating with the cable is painful. I cry, holding on to the cable with one hand and the homework I am doing with the other. I take it for a few more minutes. And he tells me we are going tomorrow to get a new TV, and I must carry it home. This is my punishment, physical labour. He warns me and orders that I return the game and not think about doing it again. I am like, whew, at least the game is intact.

I feel powerful holding that iPod in my hand. Having tried various devices, I know this is the one right here. So robust and infinite. Heaven sent to deliver me and everyone else. But as iTunes is expensive and restricted, I can only pre-load Adele early albums, for some reason. And so it is that my formative emotional worlds of love and lust happen

over songs from that British lady with a powerful voice—
going through adult break-ups. I know everything about
break-ups without having ever been in a relationship at all.
I wish I had sweet boy Stevie on my iPod—I can't flex at my
high-school mates about having Adele. But I can flex the
gadget itself, which is plenty to get me around cool places
and people.

The first girl I fall in love with, while in secondary
school, joins us much later towards the end of school. Her
name is Nyiwe. She comes at the precise moment when
Adele has been installed and activated in me. I look at her
the first time and Miss Adele plays in my ears, telling me to
watch out for this one.

I have already lost my virginity. Back when I was twelve
(admittedly quite young), I slept with the neighbour's
maid, Dakhu. She was beautiful and sexy and two years
older. She gave me looks, which sent my blood rushing into
various body parts. She was always intrigued by my doodles
in my little notebook. This led to me writing Dakhu letters,
poems. The night I lost my virginity, I knew for a fact
I was losing it to someone who had had sex before. Dakhu
told me what to do. The rest was improvised and learnt
moves I'd picked up from porn cinemas. (Why not? Such
places you will find on the outskirts of African cities.) It
was glorious. I wrote and wrote to Dakhu. If there was one
thing that propelled me into writing, it was sex. Dakhu
received some of the most descriptive erotic writing ever
produced. In none of my writing did I say I loved her. Adele

says love has got to be deep. This was pure lust. We have sex twice more before my mother intercepts my letters to her. Appalled that her son was engaging in this unholy activity, she scared the shit out of me by telling me I will get AIDS if I continue to do it. A fear that only lasted a few months.

Five years later, I meet Nyiwe. This is not just flesh feelings or lust—I picture spending time with her. That is not just sexual—she is stirring wild things in me. Nyiwe comes from a middle-class Malawian family. Like I said, locals don't like asylum seekers here, and it weighs on me how she sees me. I need to win her over.

Her place is a massive property with a fence, in a quite secluded place. On first sighting it, I remember thinking she is probably lonely around here by herself. The big question is how I shall wow her. Miss Adele offered very little in that department—she is busy rolling in the deep. My friends wow each other with fake designers. My parents are of no use to me because I have never even seen their wedding photo, and they have been together a long time. I am left with trial and error. The easiest and most sensible way is to befriend her good friend. I do just that and I am off with an ally. Every landmine and precaution shall be divulged. I have an inside girl.

I am not getting anywhere near this goal of mine. Her friends confirm with me this much. She cares nothing about sports (basketball-game invites are out of the ask) and all she is focused on right now is studying. And I, while sharing the sentiment that education is important, have spent my father's hard-earned school-fee money on the latest iPod and Adele albums. I need to get smart, or there goes my chance at true love. I am bouncing from chair to chair—through the classes. Paying classmates to switch seats with me so I can talk to her. I try everything to no avail. I am desperate now, which is not a good place to mount from. I lay my cards on the table, but not too many. I tell her I want to eat with her sometime and she says, 'Maybe.'

I have been on the maybe for so long I almost stop chasing her. But that's when I put a plan in motion. I make tremendous plans. I am always one plan away from a break-through. I will put together a collection of all my plans and get it published. Yes—this is a brilliant plan.

I make my move when she is least expecting it, Churchill style. I don't mean to make it sound unglamorous, court-ship, but it's done differently here. I deploy my letters and poems for the wow factor. They are a sure thing. I can't believe I didn't use them until now, thinking she is above them. I feel I am dangerously rolling in too deep. A hero's call to adventure and mystery. I answer. I hope she does too.

One thing you can never expect in grand planning is the abrupt shock of rejection, like lightning. It's Saturday, it's Sunday—or is it both? It is most definitely the weekend, I know that. Maybe it happened on both days. I think I felt it on both days—for multiple days. I see her for the last time, and it's like the first time, Nyiwe. I bring a hand-written letter through the dusty streets of Malawi, carrying a purple umbrella in case of acid rain. Passing Chinsapo all the way to where she lives. I've saved money for the bus ride, bought clean clothes to look good and sharp. Flowers in one hand, a letter and umbrella in the other.

I am too scared to tell her the extent of my feelings, though my spectacular outfit and flowers reveal more of my intentions than the letter ever could. I walk away, but ten minutes later I go back, determined to tell her how I feel. We are outside her compound. 'I want to remain friends with you,' Nyiwe says. I hear the words echo, like it's only the two of us on the highest peak in the hills. I'm certain she hasn't even read the letter I wrote her, carefully edited for days. But she denies it. Denies it like I made a preposterous accusation. It feels like I tempted the devil, and my punishment is painful. She walks away carrying both the flowers and the letter. Closes the gate behind her.

Thunder, lightning. Acid rain.

I think to myself, good thing I brought my purple umbrella. I am a master planner.

The anti-regime riots in Malawi, with mobs looting and storming the capital, leave my father anxious. We have just escaped one terror in Rwanda. Now, here in Malawi, it feels like we are about to experience another.

First time I remember hearing a gunshot, I am very young. I keep ending up in scenarios where I am exposed to the sound of them. Every time it happens, it feels like the first time. Close to gunshots, the sound is sharp, distinct and penetrates your ears, so you remember what it is you are hearing.

My parents, my sisters and I are ducking for cover in my parents' room while bullets fly across the roof like diagonal ice rain, but more deadly. We all know the drill, stay quiet till it all dies down. My mother, my sisters and I are curled up on the floor holding hands. My father is standing in the bedroom doorway, carrying in his hand a machete.

When this started yesterday, no one thought it would escalate this quickly. At about eleven in the morning, Mother gets a call from my father. He is in the city, resupplying for the kiosk. We are near to the city, where the riots start. His voice has an urgency; in the background you can hear the mob screaming. Something bad is about to happen, and quickly. He is instructing Mother and me to take bags of corn and beans that we have in the kiosk and put them behind doors in the house. 'Lock the windows, don't open them for anyone until I get home.'

The first night we isolate, I do not sleep, none of us do. My father is getting messages and updates from his friends. They have broken into his friend's house and terrorised them while taking everything in it. Throughout the night we hear mobs screaming, 'Go back to where you came from. You are next.'

The streets and borders are blocked, no fleeing town. We get through the night. Next day this is where we are. My father is waiting with a machete in his hand in case the mob breaks in, while the rest of us are curled around each other on the floor. The military fire at the mobs around our kiosk and house.

I look at my mother's face and see the expression I have seen my whole life. The one that says, everything will be okay. At about midday the gunshots stop. The riots cease. People have been killed over the two days. Even after, my father does not let his guard down, he still holds the machete in his hand. My mother holds my hand. And I hold Angel's. Angel holds Jo's and Jo holds Boni's. We stay like this in silence till midnight.

IV

MY FATHER RESOLVES TO RAISE me and my sisters a certain way. A Christian way. We attend Sunday school and most of the schools that my sisters and I attend are Christian run. When I graduated primary school, my parents decided that I should get into a decent secondary school. After searching, my father finds a school he thinks will be great. Close to where we live. He asks for help from a friend—otherwise known as bribing a police officer. I am accompanied by my father's friend, the police officer. He is here to make the whole thing look legit. A police officer is taken seriously. My father has the novel idea of using him and my good grades to speak volumes at the interview and allow me to be admitted to this school. It will get me where I need to go, Chinsapo Secondary School. But first I must go see a secondary-school delegator. A decider of sorts, picking the type of school students get into; imagine Ivy League school obstacles at the public level. The delegator lives in Lilongwe—we make our way there.

Walking up the stairs, I dread it. With every step, it feels like a staircase to heaven or hell. I let the police officer take the lead. I walk behind him into an office with brown shelves, and papers everywhere. I feel as if I am in a courtroom and my lawyers have instructed me not to say anything. As he talks, I imagine my father outside, trying to imagine me inside. The interview is a blank memory now, and afterwards we head out. Walking down the stairs, I know something has happened. My father's friend, the police officer, has indeed got me into a decent school given the grades I offered them. This makes my father happy. The police officer hands me over to my father and we ride back home. Goodbyes are exchanged before the engine of the Toyota Dyna ignites. Driving back, we don't say a word to each other. I watch my father drive—trying to pick up a few things here and there, like a true autodidact. I am beaming with gratitude, not sure what I should be grateful for.

Mr Zeleza wears his pants way high—cartoonishly—and a grey leather cowboy belt of some sort that goes with his black pants. He has a stern look, an efficient precision when you visit him in his office, which I do from time to time for getting in trouble. As a mathematics teacher for our class, he commands the room well. He writes very little on the board. Instead, he talks a lot; he is a drunk. Rumbling and mumbling about this and that, making sense about the subject at hand, a functional drunk. He drinks a lot, his role affording him high-end stuff. He doesn't drink the cheap alcohol Malawi can offer. Chibuku Shake! Shake!—a fermented alcohol, usually brewed at home and taken to the taverns. This beer is for other alcoholic teachers at Chinsapo Secondary School. Mr Zeleza drinks Carlsberg. Most of my maths teachers are raging alcoholics—it's a miracle I come out of school with any recognisable grades.

Mr Zeleza smells from a distance. His classes are always in the morning. He is an early drinker. And yet he is on top of his shit. When he is pissed to the maximum, he calls me to the front to write exercises on the chalkboard from his special teacher's textbook. It has answers at the back of it. I always flip to the next page and peek at the solutions. I have a reputation for being the best note-taker on campus. I get paid for it. Yes—I am niche and not getting laid a lot right now, but it will all change, you already know that. Change is always around the corner for me. I will become a sex machine.

He calls me Oliver Emmanuel because that's who I am right now. I have always been that to everyone here at school. My first name and my middle name, omitting my last name altogether. A ploy by my parents to blend in. We call all our teachers by their last names, and they don't know any of ours. Too many students in the class. Wooden desks fill the classrooms, multiple columns and rows of students. I doubt my teachers care or remember who I am and what I will become. We tease our life-skills teacher mainly because we hate the subject, not finding it worthy, wanting life changes more than skills at this age. The subject, as far as I can narrow it, comes to two fundamental tasks: girls being warned about not getting pregnant and boys being warned not to get sexually transmitted diseases.

We fail this miserably. The class of 2013 has victims of both. But not me. I will be dead if I get a girl pregnant at school. I am talking a literal death inflicted upon me by my parents. Murder of many degrees. I already hear the echoing questions: who is going to feed the baby? How are you going to earn enough money to support yourself? Why did you do this to us? I always find it funny how parents, African parents, take failure in their children as a personal slight to them. I wish to add everything to their tabs, all my personal shortcomings—but no, they are picky about it.

Back at school, in between learning how to use a condom and taking breaks, we dance, vibe and groove. This weekend, a song comes out by a Nigerian musician and it's a hit. An Afro-beat rhythm that is taking over the radio waves—'Oliver Twist'. It is the first time I hear the smooth mesh of those two words. It is a name that lends itself to something cool, something of a legend.

The second weekend of the song being out, my classmates address me as Oliver Twist. There it is, revealed to me as if it's always been there, a birthmark, a complete mark.

Mr Vale is our advanced-mathematics teacher. A branch of mathematics that is so advanced very few at school qualify for it, few being FOUR students, including me—can I be more niche? Mr Vale drinks Chibuku—the lowlife of beers. He is always drinking and often asks us, the four musketeers, to meet him at the tavern to grab our assignments. He leaves class early. He also doesn't know my original last name, given to me at birth. I feel estrangement between my peers and my teachers.

Outside these school walls, they call me Zulupapuwa. I earn this name by carrying a designer satchel to school one summer—the coolest I feel at school for sure. A leather shoulder strap, a green and red bag. I got it after crying in a marketplace. Forcing my father to buy it for me. Annoying and embarrassing him, which makes him angry.

I am glad to have found this Zulupapuwa bag in a free market in Malawi. With this on my shoulder, it will throw off my classmates—off the scent of me being a foreigner, a refugee, an unwanted immigrant, a freeloader. I want to earn my keep, and with this it's a start to that mountain hill. I go along with the name, I hold on to the bag, through its wear and tear—through forms 3 and 4 (years 11 and 12). I am Zulupapuwa here at school, at home I am Olivier. Lift me up, out of the basement, from niche to kingdom. Give me my flowers, my pride. I am of here, from here. No one will confuse me for anyone else, anything else—something other. Soon I forget who I am, soon I will forget where I come from. I have given up any hopes of getting out of here. I am sixteen years old—I stretch this moment now to eternity.

Good friends don't ask for much. Making it a kindred companionship—one fostered throughout years if you are lucky. One of my good friends I love and talk to is Patrick. I know Patrick as Precious for a long time, from school years. Chinsapo Secondary School. We meet on a basketball court gambling money with a point-shot game he always wins. He has that Kobe shot in the can, ready to go. I thought, okay. I need to learn how to do that. From the beginning, Patrick and I feed off each other. He frequents my house often, and we go on winding, waxing poetic chats. We challenge each other off and on the court. I am here on the phone with Patrick. I am in Darwin, Northern Territory (famed for crocodiles and fireworks). It's hot, we laugh and reminisce. He works and studies in China. He has been in China for the last few years. He recently moved to Wuhan, patient zero for COVID-19, the boy lives dangerously.

I think everyone from where we grew up in Malawi would agree that we felt abandoned, left on the outskirts. They don't care about what happens to us. Nothing is clearer to me than coming to Australia and observing the excess resources at people's disposal. Something sinister is running in everyone's veins here, an 'out of sight, out of mind' mentality. The average person in Malawi or Rwanda works so very hard to earn so very little.

I feel removed from it all now. Patrick works a lot too. 'Spend money, make money,' he says. 'I will rest (retire) when I am forty.' He is sending money back to his mother and sister in Malawi like the dutiful son he is. Patrick's mother was always welcoming to me when I visited Patrick at her house.

Patrick and I get to have our esteem affirmed when we meet Alex, that crossed-eyed genius. The first genius I ever met. Alex lives on the affluent side of the Chinsapo. He attended university at one of the top places to study in the country and now has a great job. He works with NGOs to start supportive initiatives. This is how we meet at Kusula Malawi, a community centre near a massive soccer playground. Their aim is to empower youth in Malawi, asylum seekers and citizens, with education. By implementing classes in French, English and Mathematics. Library and computer facilities are built next to classrooms. Patrick and I meet Alex and the Canadians (co-founders of Kusula Malawi) while we are still in school, and volunteer to help with classes and lessons. I keep in touch with Alex. Patrick and I are on the phone talking about Alex and his foresights. Grateful to have such a friend, all while I enjoy the Australian sun.

My family is attending a Pentecostal church in Chilinde in Lilongwe. I don't remember how we found it, maybe word of mouth or a fire in a bush, but we have been coming here forever. I am the vuvuzela boy at church. Before they are fashionable, I blow trumpets. Before that, I blow flute. Between praises and hymns, alongside ululations. Everyone looks at me, on the right side of the church near the band section in this intimate one-hundred-seater theatre. I am sitting on this uncomfortable pew, and next to me, a vuvuzela. A blessing from God, courtesy of the soccer world cup in South Africa. A blow for praise, I blow to raise. To all high almighties. I blow to warn Nero about the fire before the Roman empire burns to ashes. Lips puffy, lungs pumpy, I am the healthiest boy who ever lived. Ear-to-ear sound travels the room to the gates of heaven. Looping over again, seven times.

My father appears too serious. He is Bantu black and wears glasses, round unfashionable ones. But he is an excellent dancer, my father. He is a boogie man if you will. This is perhaps the only time he loosens. It is time for praise in service, and Pentecostals love to dance when praising the Lord. He takes his glasses off and everyone knows 'boogie man is getting down'. He slides his body on the red, polished, shining floors of the parish, all the way to the centre. Two steps move and everyone gives him room. And then the moment comes, knees bent, he shuffles, wiggles his bent legs, his back lower, left to right. Everyone goes crazy. They are loving my father and his dance. I feel the holy spirit passing through here—the energy is unmatched. I watch from my chair everyone rejoicing. I hold tight, ready for my moment with the vuvuzela.

The pastor and his deacons never join in on the dance floor when my father takes stage. I think it's because they don't want to embarrass themselves, though it could also be because Pastor Nkhoma has a plastic leg. The leg has been paid for by the church tithe. Since we paid the tithe at church, I suppose we paid for it. By 'we' I mean my parents. He loses a leg in a horrible car crash, and it is such a miracle that he comes through onto the other side alive. His leg is not the only expense the tithe is covering. Other expense coverages include church conventions featuring guest speakers (my parents' favourite). The cost of damages to the pastor's car, which is also the church car (the Lord's car). And also, his children's private school fees. (For God's sake, are you seeing this, God? The man is allocating your money to his everyday expenses. Does he have your blessing for this?)

I have little regard for Pastor Nkhoma evidently, or his prosperity messages. I steal money from the tithe basket. Oh God, I am such a rebel. Manifestos and scriptures will be written in my name. Vigils will be held in my absence. The tithe baskets move around—vacuuming people's deep pockets, ending up at the front of the dance floor. After tithe, it's worship time. I raise my hand, kneel on the ground in front of the pulpit. I am a sinner. Next to the basket, everyone closes their eyes except me. My hand reaches in and grabs a few notes while I'm reciting, 'Forgive our sins, Father.' Right here, I know my niche— my calling from heaven. A kleptomaniac emerges from the church, rises with the doves, and ascends into the clouds. Before you feel a type of way about this, let me add that worse things have happened in churches.

I steal money for one week and go back the next to ask for forgiveness. My father is not as forgiving as God. I steal from him and feel the wrath of steel, timber and leather. Sometimes plastic. Oh, I miss those golden years of plastic. Stealing from him is a class-A offence. One punishable to the fullest, and he takes pride in it, punishment.

I think it's miraculous, God's hand intervening right before Abraham will kill for him, take his son's life. The parable when it's shared at Sunday school is revered. The moral of the story, as I view it, is that God's love and devotion are all you need to understand, to never question. And everyone, including my teachers, overlooks the fact that a father is killing his son with his hands. It mortifies me. The love, the devotion to God. My father's devotion is no different. I am terrified of his love of God. Getting older, between growing taller and becoming braver, I catch the belt with my hand when my father swings. You should see the look on his face as I fight back. I feel something in me—godlike, I cannot quite put my finger on it. And with this, he punishes me more. He makes me sit on the cement floor of the house for hours. Sometimes he wants me kneeling on it until he closes the kiosk, hours on my knees—my joints are feeling detached from my body. My mother watches me through the agony. She never defies him. I resent her for this, not knowing we are both prisoners of his making.

I mostly go to church to hang out with friends until I discover girls. Church girls. With my newfound love of them my devotion to Jesus goes through the roof, but trying to impress Christian girls is an ongoing, endless ladder. 'Do you love God?' is their returning question, to which I always respond, 'Yes, my dear. Why wouldn't I? He brought me to you.'

The deacon of our Pentecostal church has a cute daughter who I try to hang out with. I visit their house, staying for dinner and offering to help around the house if needed, to become their errand boy. I don't get anywhere though, and after a three-day weekend church convention I attend, my chances of winning her over are decimated.

Church conventions are some of the best times in my life. I love attending them, trading stories around bonfires, hanging out with everyone, and sleeping over the entire weekend. A commune gathering that has lasted the test of time in religion. It's basically like the Splendour in the Grass festival, or any other festival, with minor differences. Tents are built near the church along with bathrooms, though less robust compared to those at Splendour. We take group showers while smacking each other's bums like kids do (not offered at Splendour). In the morning we eat a meal that's been prepped for everyone, same with lunch. At Splendour you buy your meals, and they are pricey. Should I keep going?

After all the festivities and church service, and fire chat and stories, it's bedtime.

The festival finishes with a bang on Sunday. I am already excited on Friday night. It's been a wonderful first day of the convention. We share humorous PG-rated anecdotes around the bonfire while sipping on tea. Bedtime comes and I am nervous because my bladder is flaky. I am so nervous that I keep waking up in the middle of the night to check my mat. I make it to Saturday morning—dry season. I spend the day fetching firewood for the night's stories, excited to share a few of my own. Then I go to bed. But on this night, the night before the big day—Sunday—my bladder fails me.

I wet the shirt I've worn to bed, the same shirt I wanted to wear on Sunday for the big close because it's a good shirt and the only clean one I brought. I was lying close to a pile of clothes next to my mat and so I soak everything. I take the shirt to the church and throw it on a pile of clothing for ironing, hoping no one notices it's wet and just irons it. In the past, when the duties of ironing clothes fell onto me, I would have gotten away with this, but not today. Five minutes later, after piling my shirt on top of other clothes, a guy who I will forever hate comes out of the back door of the church and announces, 'Whose shirt is this? I can't iron this shirt, it's wet. Pee, I think. Oliver, didn't you wear this yesterday?' And right then I felt the universe transpiring to curse me. At a church of all places.

Everyone finds out about it that Sunday morning, the girls, the whole dang church. I walk in shame and refuse to go to church as frequently from then on.

On the block, word is that my father has AIDS. This is not true—I will bury them for saying that.

My mother told me he has it, that's how the rumour spread. My guess is, she is not happy with him.

Thank goodness the word stays on the block. If it makes its way to school or church, I am done for. The child of an AIDS carrier? No—not in this lifetime. Try again in the next, maybe. I will bury them if they laugh at me. Laugh at my father. It's not a laughing matter. I decide what is funny. I will heckle if they start with me on that shit. Fuck them. I will clown their arses. They call him and us Maburundi. We are not even Burundians. Basic idiots, these Malawians. Ignoramuses. It's appalling. I don't need this. I see them, their eyes eager and full of an insatiable appetite. They want to know about our business—not for profit. To pass the time. The lazy people. The worst gossips. If they laugh about my beating from my father when I wet the bed, I will bury them, every single one of them. I will run them over with my father's Dyna truck. If they laugh at his sickness,

I will bury them, then raise them from the dead, only to bury them again. And then piss on their graves. They don't know him and how he became like this. They don't know us and our story, don't deserve our story, don't deserve us.

My father's sickness feels cold, snow-like, I imagine. London maybe, or New York. No, Russia. Yes, Russian cold snow with vodka. He is weak but doesn't let on. And now, because of his condition and where it will lead him, I become the man of the house. Do I? Am I? Am I a man? The man. My family, my church, my father and my mother hope for a man with a capital M. I show weakness. I take too long to decide. I consider every move before committing. I hesitate. You cannot hesitate in wartimes, genocidal times, conflict times, survival times. I don't meet them at their level. I come up short. Shame engulfs me. Strangles my neurons. I think I am incomplete. An incomplete thought.

I am around when his friends come to visit him. He makes these trips to the hospital. On meds now. Many meds, I don't know. He doesn't talk about them. I wonder though. How long he has, how long until I am thrust into the tornado of adulthood that awaits me. My mother knows what awaits me. I see it on her sombre face. She wants to say he is too young but says nothing. I imagine all this. Women outlive men where I am from. It's terrifying for me. But what is asked of me, will it go to my mother? I doubt she wants to be a man or knows what that means. My mother is taking care of him while running the kiosk. I give in and ride the bike to buy Coca-Cola for the kiosk—an errand boy. My physical strength is all I offer. What is the point of having a son, after all? Coca-Cola is a big sale item in humid central African summers and resupplying is a bitch of a process. We have bottles and bottles in the fridge. A common mode of transport in Malawi is walking. Well, not much of a mode, more like nature. It's free, and if you are healthy, you can get good at it. I start with carrying crates in my hand and on my head. Walking to a container near a Coca-Cola delivery factory. The key is to get there early and line up. Two crates are the maximum since I carry them on my head. Others go three. They have fat giraffe necks, these people. After a few years, I upgrade to a bicycle. An actual mode of transport. This one requires great riding skills. I ride back to my father's weak body in bed, thinking of how long he would have done this for. His back is bad for it.

My father is suffering from homesickness. There is no cure for that now. We are refugees, after all. We are sick of being away from home, trying to chase the feeling of seeing the people you know and love. End-of-day joy. Removed from millions of people, in a single wipe. Blast.

Another sickness he suffers from is diabetes. I am not sure whether it's type one or two. I assume the latter. I think from too much cola-drinking. He loves sugar (sukali), in a very concerning way. He is not taking insulin. He is not on a kidney dialysis. I wonder if it's because he cannot afford it. Now he's in his mid-fifties, give or take, my father's condition is worsening. At the start he walks fine, drives fine and you'd better watch yourself on the dance floor. In the middle, he stays home and hides. In the end, he still stays home but can't hide anymore. He is at his very tail end.

I am about to graduate from high school. Chinsapo Secondary School has its perks, but it is a pain in my arse. I find the school painful. My father's sickness is not getting better, and he is counting on me to come through, flying colours, rainbow style. Did it rain? Raining man, but I am a boy. It's the last hope, his plan, which he lays out to me after a recent visit to one of his friends. In the Nissan, he tells me how Jerome's son is going to Canada. How? I think. There is a program for refugees, a way out of the shit-hole situation we are trapped in this moment. World University Services of Canada, WUSC, is the name of the program. It allows you (me) to go to Canada on a scholarship. And like the rocket that will take all people to the next planet, I am expected to get honours and get this one-way ticket for everyone out of here. The gravity of my situation is not considered. Crabs-in-a-bucket style. But the fear is, and has always been, which is all imaginary now, that I will go over and be the lost son, the one that forgets where he comes from.

All talk of this and that, vagabond hopes—it might never eventuate, not this way. So, when my father is explaining what it takes to get there, when and how it will happen for our family, he is super certain. It's not hopes and dreams of the immigrant. It's Moses and faith. It's a prophecy. I am to go there to end a generational struggle. His words are certain yet scary, time's arrow—Canada. He is dying. He knows it perhaps more than anyone, even God—like Bowie knew, like the knight in *The Seventh Seal,* like we all will during our last moments. He feels it—death. The Blackstar. So, while there is no 'will' that delegates who gets what when he dies, he imparts a spiritual will. And like a prophet receiving instructions from God, I follow them to the end. A few months after this conversation, he will remind me again, as I enter my final year of secondary school. Go hard or go nowhere. He is getting sicker and sicker. His vomits and coughs will be diagnosed as tuberculosis.

V

YOU DON'T GET TO CHOOSE which country you go to when you are a refugee seeking resettlement. But you are told who wants you in advance so you can start getting ready. In the winter of 2012, Canada has taken an interest in my family's case. I am thrilled, I have heard great things about Canada. A lot of refugees leaving Dzaleka go there.

Canada and Rwanda are both French-speaking colonies. If I end up there, we can bond over how non-threatening a coloniser speaking French is. I don't know about you, but I have never been shaken to my core by the words of a French person. My mother would love it there too. Her French is better and the rest of us would brush up on ours.

Resettlement is a long process. With Canada, we go all the way to the last stage. Which is an interview with Canadian Immigration right here in Dzaleka. The morning of the interview, my family and I dress up nicely. We get to the upper side of the camp where the UN offices are. This is where they interview people. We walk inside the waiting room. We are the last family on the interview list. The interviews take a long time. I pick up a UNICEF magazine on the table to pass time. The front page reads, 'Madonna adopts son from Malawi'. Damn it, I think to myself, that could have been me. I am a wordsmith. I can help her write songs. I write them, she sings them. The next best duo, unstoppable.

'Olivier, Olivier.' My mother interrupts my daydream with my stepmother Madonna.

'What, Mother?!' I answer back.

'Let's go, we have been called in, put the book down . . .'

We go inside and I see them, 'azungu'. So much is depending on them.

They ask me, Angel and Jo what we are. We say, 'HUTU', and then, after a few introductory questions, they send us outside. They are about to question my parents about the genocide. They send us, the children, out of the room to preserve our innocence. What innocence? By fourteen years old I have been exposed to unbelievable things that makes a grownup out of a child. Things that rob any child of their innocence.

Outside the interview room, Madonna and I pick up where we left off. I live vicariously through the boy. The boy from the land of flames, the boy who harnesses the wind.

Months after the interview, I am in the living room waiting. We have this vintage TV here and I am watching an old British comedy show called *Mind Your Language*. It's a show about immigrants taking English night classes. I am in the middle of an episode when my father calls me. 'Olivier, come here.' He wants me to do something for him. He is holding a letter in his hands, UNHCR stamped on it. I open the letter and start reading it.

Department of Immigration Canada. 'Dear Seba. We regret to inform you, we will not be proceeding further with your application for resettlement . . . while your case is pressing, we believe there is not sufficient information.'

Not 'sufficient information'? What the hell does that mean?! Sufficient information: how about a father and mother with four kids and no way to feed them. Sufficient information: how about escaping persecution every place we go? Sufficient information: how about living in terror with locals who don't want us here?

After graduating high school at seventeen years old, I have good grades. I have that opportunity my father was hoping I would gain. I have a chance of applying for a scholarship through WUSC. If I go through, I get a visa and I can bring my family over. It's the last chance for my family to resettle and start again.

I go through the first stage of the application. The second part of the application involves taking a test. Five questions on the test. One of the question is 'Where do I see myself in five years?' which is a huge ask of anyone, let alone a seventeen-year-old refugee. 'Where do I see myself in five years?' Ah, anywhere but here.

I proceed to the interview stage, my second time facing Canadian Immigration. Only difference this time, it's just me. And I am after a scholarship on merits. A few weeks after the interview, I receive a letter from WUSC. I open the letter and start reading. 'World University Service of Canada. Dear Olivier, we regret to inform you . . .'

A year and a half before arriving in Australia is when I found out my father was sick. He had lost a lot of weight. With his age, it took a toll on him. He ended up spending a lot of time at home in the last days. One morning, things worsened.

My mother wakes me up at four in the morning. It is cold, unusually cold. Nordic. I am half-asleep and see her fidgeting while packing her handbag. She tells me to put on clothes. We are going to the hospital. The car is on the way. My heart immediately starts beating a million times faster. I quickly get everything together. I help her with getting him in the car. My father's head is resting on my shoulder in the back seat of the car.

We pull into Emergency. They wheel him in, all the way into the operating room. I am standing outside the operating room. Everything feels very surreal. My parents' friends are here. About two hours pass. My mother and the doctor come out. They tell me he is stable, in a diabetic coma.

My mother stays with him, and I go attend to my sisters. At home I tell Angel and Jo that our father is in the hospital, but he is okay. We all wait. It feels longer than our fourteen years' wait for resettlement. Evening comes and I hear cars pull over outside our compound. I hear my mother crying as I open the door and right then I know. Slowly the reality seeps into my sisters' eyes. They too start crying.

There're too many people here. I need to be alone. I isolate myself in the kiosk, I walk to the chair that he used to sit at all the time. I take a moment, to let it sink in. I wish this chair was next to his bed in his last moment and I could be there with him. I want to hold his hand. The hand that for as long as I can remember held three things only: money, a bible and a machete. I want to say to him while I hold his hand, I forgive you. You can rest in peace now.

When my father dies, it is the church that arranges the funeral—it's customary. We don't have blood family here in Malawi, who I am sure would have loved to be here to say goodbye and help us through our grief. When the casket with my father goes down, so does the nature of his beliefs. Such is clear, without a doubt. A eulogy given by our bishop—and there he goes. A tombstone with a name on it.

A week after the funeral, my mother goes on a worship tour, visiting every evangelical and Pentecostal convention, donating money as tithe—asking for blessings. She is praying and praying, asking God for our family's salvation. Asking God for a one-way ticket. Asking for our family to be next in selection for the resettlement with UNHCR Malawi.

We must return to Dzaleka after my father's death. We're running away. Running from the debt collectors, from landlords and tax agents, running away from capitalism itself. Funeral costs and money my father owes—borrowed to purchase his three-tone Toyota Dyna truck—force us into a tight corner of disabling debt. My mother sells the truck and uses half the money to help repay the debt. Education for my sisters comes to an abrupt stop. I have just graduated from secondary school in Chansapo in Lilongwe. Now we've got to go, leave. I don't leave willingly. We pack everything, which is not much, and head back.

We drive back to the camp over hills and zigzag roads with the most striking view of bare land. Forgetting how fertile it can get, one notices a sadness to it, a longing air of despair and pain among the people. Over thirty thousand people crammed together waiting like dead, soon-to-be-fallen leaves or flowers, waiting to be picked or taken to the trash. We, my family and I, are waiting to be picked, selected by nations that don't prioritise our wellbeing. Left to fend for ourselves.

In Dzaleka, my mother can't open a kiosk like we did in Lilongwe. She has no disposable income to invest in this kind of business. The bank has denied us credit. Denied us legitimacy. The only hope we have is UNHCR. 'Any time now,' my mother says. 'Okay, Mother,' I say back. She thinks of how she is going to stretch the money we have until the golden tickets arrive in the mailbox. The metaphorical mailbox—we don't have addresses here, or mailboxes.

In the camp, a man I meet called Remy is also waiting for the golden ticket that comes via airlines (sometimes paid for, often not) when resettlement is approved. He has been here a long time, like many of us, and I meet him by chance when I visit his store. Unbeknownst to me, he knows of me from the time my family and I spent in Dzaleka before getting an exit permit for Boni. Remy is the older guy in a prison that can get his hands on anything you need if you offer him something in return. I don't use prison lightly here. A camp can be animalistic, medieval and very Dickensian, Darwinian even, in the worst sense of 'survival of the fittest'. Remy runs several somewhat legitimate businesses, and I am about to get on his payroll.

A lucrative business in Dzaleka offers services: internet cafés, restaurants, cinemas or fixing things. Remy is a fixer: a jack of all trades, like me. He has a kiosk of his own and he fixes electronics of all sorts. I remember thinking, this guy is smart. I am blown away by his charm and wit. A slow talker who knows too much about the cosmos, you would think he is a personal assistant to Carl Sagan himself. Remy is Congolese, speaks fluent English. He is a student at the only college here in Dzaleka. His business is profitable, and he is the man they come to when something needs fixing.

Back in the Lilongwe city I know men like Remy. Men like Francis, a bootlegger and a fantastic bullshitter, a lying sack. Not even elaborate lies—fragile short-lived anecdotes about the origin stories of famous entrepreneurs. 'That's how Bill Gates started, bro,' he says one time, and I respond rhetorically, 'Bill bootlegged at Harvard?'

Francis runs a studio, a bootlegging studio house where people record music periodically. His kiosk is next to my room and the noise can be unbearable when I am trying to sleep. But at the chance of working for Francis and making a little money, I jump at it and he takes me under his wing, and I bootleg and sell files on DVDs, CDs and flash disks.

Francis and Remy, like many dealers of content and entertainment in Malawi and many parts of Africa, thrive on the geo-restrictions of entertainment-distribution and intellectual-property laws. Exploiting these loopholes and maximising profit is what I am employed to do. The act of devaluing art, copying. Francis has huge hard drives, containing music, shows, photos and films. I frequented Francis's kiosk when the previous owner, also a dealer, let me work for him. Francis worked for him too, which is how we meet. Operating in a front kiosk doing file transfers to customers' storage devices, it's a simple job for easy money. The owner's name is Rafiki, a freakishly tall South African man who moved to Malawi a few years back.

Rafiki is a rough guy from the slums of Soweto—he never forgets to remind me of his horrific upbringing. He is stubborn too, doesn't want to expand the business to anything more than music and film, keeps it PG-rated. He is a man of God. Exactitude and order are important to Rafiki. When I work for him, he instructs me to never use short-cuts. No 'control + v' or 'control + c'. 'There are no short-cuts in life,' he says—always saying it with a deep voice, imitating a 'eureka' monk moment. An enlighten-ment moment.

Francis and I, both working for Rafiki, are tired of his limitations. We execute a takeover, a plan. A master plan. I am so good at planning. My plan is to save money and buy new computers and kick Rafiki out of business, which works amazingly. Francis and I have a reign only matched by the pharaohs.

Back in Dzaleka, Remy hears all about my experience at our informal interview. I have brought with me to camp all my content from Lilongwe on my laptop. I offer him an opportunity to expand his business into the realm of explicit content for more customers and more money. Remy is a smart entrepreneur, sees my plan, thinks it over, and boom! I am hired. Thus begins my job of bootlegging, selling porn and content in Dzaleka refugee camp. At the ripe, fresh age of seventeen.

At seventeen years old, bootlegging porn is, for me, a much-needed hustle, something to look forward to. A way to gather stories to tell my friends Gasore, John and Samuel. Also, learn a thing or two for my lovely ladies. My mother, goodness bless her soul, doesn't ask where the money is coming from. Nor does she condemn that which stems from dirt. For now, while waiting is dragging, this day-to-day hustle will do, the very hustle that brings some money to my mother. I strongly sense she knows. Not to the extent, but she knows.

Remy normally opens the kiosk and closes it as well—a task for me these days. On a sunny day, windy as, I open the kiosk. I catch a smell of fresh dirt from last night's rain. Fresh air blowing my way. Various people come past the kiosk—friends, family or customers. I switch personas mid-sale as if I have multiple personalities. Switching from 'a cordial smile' for friends and family to 'pensive stare' for customers, being indifferent while they decide between hard-core porn sub-categories videos. Flipping and switching gears from a regular person to a guy you can't negotiate with—no bargains on porn, it's like a bail fee. Once set, it must be met.

My sister Jo pays me a visit one time—the timing is terrible as I am with a customer who is eagerly perusing a popular porn category of 'farmer wants a wife.' This is the closest my family gets to finding out what I do. Jo got into a fight at school, and she is almost in tears. While she has physically been in battle, mine is internal—I am panicking inside. Folders and folders of archival porn are stored on this computer. She stands at the front of the kiosk, recalling events leading up to the fight. My peripheral focus is closing tabs on my laptop, one category after another, telling customers to excuse me. Jo's story is reaching its climax and she finishes. I console her, tell her to go home. Whew, I dodge one fast bullet. And so, the hustle continues.

A friend of mine, Gasore, who is an aspiring mogul and community leader, tells me a story about a hero of his, Jay-Z. He says Jay-Z started as a hustler and used to sell drugs to his neighbours, friends, and family even, where he grew up in Marcy Projects in New York. Jay-Z is a billionaire now. I remember thinking, wow, me and Jay-Z are cut from the same cloth: he deals drugs and I deal porn. Both are addictive. Our paths, mine and Jay-Z's, have not aligned yet. Jay-Z has over a billion-dollar net worth, and I am now in my mid-twenties with a lot of money tied up in potential. The reason, the difference between us, I like to think, is in our principles. When he was selling drugs in the projects Jay-Z would always say 'Never get high on your own supply,' which rhymes (mogul, dealer, and rapper, just wow). And I, well, I was getting high on my supply, if you catch my drift.

My mother is not loving my disappearing acts, waking up in the morning, going to the kiosk and working for Remy. If she knew what I was selling, she would be fuming. I disappear and only come back for lunch. Which would be fine for a working person bringing in a considerable amount of money, but as Remy takes the lion's share of profits, I end up not keeping much. It's a labour of love, I tell myself. These Houdini disappearing acts, coupled with my long nights out, are stirring a different side of my mother I have not seen before. She says I am acting like my own man and not her child. Tension builds.

In Dzaleka people stay out late, as if to remind themselves tomorrow is the same shit, anyway. Why rush to dream? Rush to wake? We have been here for a long time. Moon dreaming, dreaming about moonwalking, about moon landing. It will change nothing. As if things will change drastically overnight. People stay up, and I do too. Walking home after trading tales. Gasore, John and Samuel are my comic relief. The moon is clear and bright, any clearer and wolves will howl through the alleyways of huts in Dzaleka camp. It is a moon in a horror film.

It is close to midnight when I get home and find that my mother has closed the door. Opening it, I hear her get up from the bedroom. We sleep in one room, all of us. Five, to be exact, all lying on one mattress we brought with us from Lilongwe. It's uncomfortable enough to sleep and share this small space, let alone be woken up from it. She hears me coming through the door close to midnight for the third

94

time this week, and it's not even Thursday. She is fed up, stepping around my sisters so as not to wake them up. She sees me and collects herself, sighs and lets out, 'I told you, if you are going to keep coming home late, you are going to need to find a place of your own.'

I know this tune. My father sang it before her. It annoys me. She sings it again like a broken record. I don't mean to, but I do fall to her level. Surprising myself too, I scream, 'I can't find my own place! I don't know anyone here. I live with you guys.'

She looks at me as her eyebrows slowly refuse to believe me at all. And then, diplomatically, she says, 'Well, I am fed up . . .'

At this point Angel, Jo and Boni wake up on the uncomfortable bed. I pity them. I freeze momentarily considering this new unfolding, I lower my voice. 'I went to the cinema, then Gasore and I hung out chatting until late.'

She looks away as if something else catches her eyes' attention, like spreading fire, more potent as it gains traction. And then, her gaze back to me, I see the fire in her eyes. She asks, 'Are you drunk?'

What! I am too insulted to answer. I don't answer her. My mother, realising that my sisters have fully woken up, wanting to put this whole thing and everyone to bed, says in a lower voice, 'I have told you before that it's stupid.' And she has, but it isn't. 'You never listen. Well—this is it! I want you to pack and leave.' It's delivered in a monotone, a plain statement. Not swaying anyone, yet permeating.

Her tone is new to my ears, familiar though, like a talk-show host attempting sincerity, landing at me in that shockingly disappointing manner when you realise you are not walking away with closure. A let-down moment at the end of a road, the end of an era.

She has said this to me so many times before. A line rehearsed, this is where the director says cut and we do this scene again tomorrow, right? No, it's opening night, the house is ready. I don't believe it hearing it now. I freeze, waiting for her other words to melt and warm the tension created in the room. And after what feels like five minutes she says it again, like an actor's rehearsed line landing magically at 'pack and leave', sounding more gut-wrenching the second time. I look at my sisters, expecting a lifeline, a lifeboat, any kind of life from them. They don't object at all. How can they? I am the man of the house, after all. 'Fine,' I rumble, this word coming out of my mouth like a fighter retreating frantically to their corner in surrender after taking too many punches. 'Fine' is all I say. I want to say things. Recite a love poem. Defend my voyeurism. I want to scream from my boxing corner, defeated, 'I am your only son!' And 'I am sorry, Momma.' But pride, ego and more untutored feelings get the best of me tonight, so I grab a duffle bag and pack. Candlelight illuminating the room, I see my sisters' eyes staring at me, in a kind of 'Oli, why did you not listen to our mother? Why are you not an obedient child?'

I am standing in the dark, cold outside. I hear wind hissing—whispering something to me. I am about to join them in nature. At this instant, I am homeless in a refugee camp. I feel abandoned, left to fend for myself even further. How selfish of her, how cold and heartless. I glance at her for mercy as the door closes and nothing is returned. 'Fine' being the last word exchanged between us. I hold tight to my bag of clothes and shiver, make my way out of the fence. In front of the fence door, I wait a few seconds. I wait for hope, for a change. I watch candlelight illuminating the living room through the little space underneath the door, then the light moves, and so do the body's shadows. My mother walks through to the bedroom. I watch through a tiny bedroom window, the only window in the hut. I watch the light occupy the room. And a slight blow of wind descends over the candle, from my mother's mouth—a wish. Outside the hut, a vast blow of chilly wind ascends my spine, giving me shivers down it. Spine. My knuckles grip tighter on my bag of belongings. Mist and smoke from my mouth. The weather commands me and I follow its direction; a wind of destruction and I am implicated—an accomplice. All the way out of the compound, through the alley, to alleys built out of dry grass. And the wind passes through them as well. It seems no one is exempt from its hisses tonight.

Wild dogs roam around the camp all the time with no one to claim them. People leave crumbs of food around the streets for the wild dogs to eat. Like the boogie man,

everyone knows the dogs exist but pay them no mind—
they're like foxes in other countries. I would, now and then,
look at them and think, their colours are different. You can
tell which ones are the hungriest. They are like the men,
women and children who jump on boats and risk it all,
whose colours always change. Whose shape will shift to fit
the mould. Blend in.

Back in Cyangugu, colours of Lake Kivu change all the
time. It's such that when there is an eruption of a volcano
that drips to the lake, a farmer rethinks that year's harvest.
It all changes, out of our control. Maybe it is bloody or
green or fluorescent, psychedelic even. The point is it keeps
changing. Patience differs from waiting around. I wonder,
looking at the stars in the sky in Dzaleka refugee camp
this lonely night. Every time one would fall, I think one
person is leaving soon to go abroad. We all blow on the
same candles and make the same wishes. They become
singular. Wishing to go to the promised land. Where
money grows on trees, and bees don't bite. I dream of
a night when I won't weigh up whether to eat lunch or
dinner. Fraudulent economics of poverty upon poverty.

In the cold in Dzaleka I gaze at the moon as if it can
offer me options, an eager spectator awaiting magic. With
the bag of clothes in my hand. I am trying to stay awake.
The cold lends an ear, I have nothing to say. I don't know
many people here in the camp. My father has done this to
me before—kicked me out of the house—but I figured she
was above it. The lesser of two evils. In the cold, my face

feels beyond pale. Blood stopping, I can't feel myself. I turn to the only man I know well in Dzaleka, well enough to help me. A person I am indebted to in this patchy period— my boss, Remy.

I show up at Remy's house with escapist trembles and he can tell straight away that something is amiss. A refugee camp is the last place to go to if you are looking to escape from family. People escape many things to come here. The only person allowed to give an alarming knock on someone's door in the middle of the night in a refugee camp is a prisoner on the run. That would be a head turner. No one shows up at your doorstep with bags and luggage having been kicked out by a family member.

Remy opens the door of his hut. The wind passes through me to him and then goes inside. And yet, like a comfortable local having a beer at his favourite bar, he is calm. Calm and collected, he watches me hold tight the only belongings I have in my bag, and with that gentle smile on his face he says, 'Well, come on in, my brother.' I take one step on the two stairs between me and the door, and on the second step I am welcomed with warmth, comfort and grace. Grateful for a friend such as Remy.

I go to work first thing in the morning. Remy has established a routine. I wake up and I see him because we are both sleeping in his bed. And while his hospitality is enormous, he minces no words in placing a value on working my hardest to remedy my situation. I am not just going to be coasting off his good will forever. He wants to make sure I know that. By asking to stay with Remy here, I have asked him to be a go-between, a mediator between my mother and I. Officiating a match, you are well versed in it at this stage, but Remy doesn't know the depth of grievances between my mother and I. Deep-rooted issues. She wants me to be the man of the house. I want to be the boy—a voyeur—a bootlegger of the camp. My father has never been chippy about being the man of our house. A role offered to me relentlessly. Why should I follow that which is condemned to misery? I don't want my family to loathe me, the way they did my father.

It's been a little over a month living with Remy. I wonder if my mother misses me. I wonder if I miss my mother. I do miss my sisters. Angel and Jo come past Remy's kiosk, bringing food from the World Food Program, my share from my mother's. It is her way of saying she cares for me. I can care for myself, I think. I take the food and give it to Remy. Food shows up periodically in the camp. People go hungriest in the gaps before and after. Time goes quickly and slowly—it's prison and we are waiting for parole with a pending riot around the corner. Filling up time in a refugee camp is a skill best learnt early on, to protect yourself from a kind of delusional psychosis that arises from thinking perhaps 'help' is coming.

Remy's generosity is dwindling like a smouldering fire. Soon he will say, 'Let's go talk to your mother and see if we can sort this out.' And soon I agree. We start the negotiations, and I don't have leverage. I have nothing to offer her to let me back into the house. I am not a changed man. I am not a man. I am still a boy. The same boy she dressed in US-flag-matching baby clothes as a child. At our mediation, I am wearing matching khaki shorts and t-shirt. Remy is taking the lead in talking to her and relaying how sorry I am. I am not. I can't remember sorry being said between my mother and I, but we patch this up with what's left of our relationship, and I move back in.

My mother has become good at picking and not picking. Mainly not picking who I can date, with me being under her roof all these years growing up. 'She is a gold digger,' my mother said of Eunice. 'And she has AIDS,' she added. She blesses people with AIDS like it's an *Oprah* giveaway. She would always throw this on top of whatever she didn't agree with in the girls I dated.

My father never cared what girls I hung out with. He was more concerned about the boys I hung out with. Were they smoking or drinking? Yes, and yes. Were they corrupting my young mind? Yes, as well. Malawian or Rwandese? Both. To be trusted with food? No. Rich or poor? Somewhere in the middle. Maybe they were filling me with dreams that would never come true. The last being a decider of not getting too comfortable. He would always say, 'Remember, Olivier, your friends' families are rich, and they have different choices.' It took little for me to adopt my father's feeling of equating money with that which could not be bought by it or any other currency.

I am dating a girl who will officially become my first proper girlfriend. Her name is Yvette. She is poor and Congolese, so I guess no objections from my mother. This is made clear by my mother because, for a change, she does not bad-mouth Yvette at all when she finds out about her. 'Be careful, Olivier,' she says now. I think she means to use a condom. Telling without being explicit about it. A unique wording. A filtered and self-policing vocabulary. At this time of my life, where she should make me feel comfortable and good around in the world, she is tongue-tied.

I meet Yvette at the camp when I come back. She has apparently always been here, but we have never met. Her energy is exciting. We are immediately sexually attracted to each other. She is a year younger and about to graduate secondary school. Everyone knows everyone in the camp. Linking us to a striking courtship. I am working at Remy's bootleg shop, and she comes to see me. We take walks to the hills nearby, outside the camp. It's nice and quiet. We date for a few months, before some unexpected news puts an abrupt stop to our relationship and thus, we say our goodbyes.

African nations, because of colonial oppression, have no infrastructure that is sustainable, economic or otherwise. Lilongwe, though poor, excites me—life exists here. Energy propels the workers, hustlers and survivors. A feeling I appreciate more with time passing. People move and I move with them; it feels like we are going places. Going places—that core elusive momentum to a refugee's existence. For to be a refugee is to move, which is to stay alive.

People wonder often about a vagabond's predicament and ask 'why?' after hearing about European, Australian or North American borders clogged with refugees. The wonders rise. 'Why in the first place would they move?' Because motion is a modality of life where I come from. To stay alive, to feel alive. A possibility of moving, legal or illegal, willingly or forced.

A volcano of refugees erupts, a wave of arrivals enters and crosses arbitrary borders and lines on maps to become some news anchor's filler story between the weather forecast and a trending topic of the week. 'In today's news, fleeing the Sudan conflict, new arrivals survive the Mediterranean Sea in search of a better life in Europe. And then we will look at some light weather coming our way, it's going to be a beautiful summer.' All while forgetting the reason motivating these people, giving them momentum, the same reason that gives anyone energy. To stay alive, to feel alive.

I am here in Lilongwe again. The capital. Breathing the air, I inhale, not noticing whether it's clean. I don't know the difference, don't know better. For I have not been to Berlin or Paris. Oh, what a precious commodity it is, how fresh. Pass me that cannabis cigarette so I can breathe. Clean air is a gem in a congested city. Here I am, on a mission my mother has sent me. The kind run by men of the house back home, the ones to do with handling money. My mother wants me to change some American dollars into Malawian kwacha so we can buy food. So we can keep on living, surviving. The city has immense possibilities and I love metropolitan lifestyle. I am romantic about it, pedantic even—a city must have a good independent library, a great African restaurant that plays music (not required but a bonus) and a wonderful city must inspire, always.

I am what you call city folk. I was born near a quiet place. Near a lake where most people farm around the villages, with clean air, and an enjoyment of a simple life with nothing but the essentials. Even though that sounds lofty, it's pure joy. Now though, as an adult, city noise helps me think. Or not think. I forget which one. I make work for people, audiences, and that's where they hang out, in the city. To channel their sounds, I need to be around their buzz. It has crossed my mind to do some work for the villagers. Maybe somewhere in the slums or favelas. I'll put this in my planner.

In Lilongwe, I recall that I have been here before with my father a handful of times, exchanging American dollars to get the kwacha currency. But I don't remember it well. Being here by myself, I want him to guide me through it all. To tell me I am headed in the right direction and that I should trust my intuition; that great danger is further away than I think; that if they chase us, wanting to rob us and take our money, we'll just jump in the car and start driving away. But none of that is true for me. I hold this bag of money close to my chest. Not wanting to squander all efforts and labour made by him for our family.

The ride back to Dzaleka on the minibus is a nostalgic ride for me. I have taken it countless times through the under-developed roads from Lilongwe to Dowa, but this time it is different. I am holding in my hands my family's fortune. Protecting it and guiding myself through the roads. After the bus, I am catching a ride, which I pay for with money already separated before I left so as to not touch the current bag of money. A ride an hour east to Dzaleka, through the winding zigzag roads, through the walks where I shall seek solace and romance. An undertaking of pleasure that makes me forget I am in this situation. I get home and deliver the money in one piece.

A few weddings, funerals and interviews later, we board a plane heading to Australia. 'A prayer answered' is my mother's exact phrasing when Australian Immigration takes us in. The best news we could all hope for. That morning my mother took a phone call in the bedroom, and she came out with a distinct face altogether, joy all over it. I felt her spread it around the room, that infectious smile of hers.

She tells us the good news and it's all wonderful. We spend the morning discussing what we need for our journey to Australia. It's not huge to us, not yet, we have become too used to this. Until we arrive there and partake in our new lives, all that is on my face is excitement and confusion.

My apologies. I'm struggling to word it in a way you understand. To know what it is like to be told your life is about to change and for that to mean something. Mean everything. Recently, I was at LAX airport coming from Paris, going to Sydney—and I saw them, the family that had just been resettled. I had time to really watch them because we were going through security. If you have not been to a strip club but have been to any American airport, it is the same experience. As I am putting my clothes and shoes back on after stripping them for very little money, I see a lady who is a caseworker for this family. She has a card around her neck with IOM on it, the International Organisation for Migration, and quickly I look over my shoulder and see the boy, see myself in the boy. He has no clue of what is ahead of him. And I am so thrilled looking at him with his family, knowing what I knew when I waited with IOM bags with my family at Brisbane Airport in July 2014. That night, I knew and understood that the worst was truly behind me.

Before we left Dzaleka we needed to pack, but first we needed fresh bags, new clothes, new everything. My mother and I enter a kiosk in Lilongwe to a mother who has a son my height and who she wants to surprise with a suit. Her son is not with her. She begs to borrow me momentarily and try the suit. I stand next to the mannequin, and we are a match. Somewhere on a security camera in Lilongwe city, a kiosk holds footage of me reluctantly trying on a suit. Shortly afterwards, we get what we came for. Bags and new clothes.

Going back to Dowa from Lilongwe on the errand my mother sent me for the first time, after countless times being on this road, I notice the airport. We are close to the airport in Dzaleka. All we needed were tickets. Of which mine and my family will read: Kamuzu > Johannesburg > Sydney and, our destination, > Brisbane. One-way with Qantas.

Through the intercom at the airport in Lilongwe comes a voice, rushing me through my goodbyes. A few more sounds and it's boarding time. Plastic bags printed with IOM all over them. I pinch, crimp, and hold the bags as they contain proof of a new beginning. This here is the last story told of its kind.

VI

WHEN WE ARRIVE AT BRISBANE Airport, my family and I have gone through an ordeal getting there. From Kamuzu Airport to Johannesburg Airport to Sydney Airport, all the way to Brisbane. All in the last thirty hours. Everyone is tired. We are waiting for an agent from the resettlement agency to take us to our new home.

At Johannesburg Airport they don't let us on the plane because my mother has in her purse 'Super Black', a hair product that makes your afro pop, a very popular product in the African diaspora. The type of hair product Michael Jackson would have used during his black years. My mother loves putting it on me and my sisters, she has fifteen tubes of them in her purse. Customs stop us and tell us: you cannot bring this on the flight. And my mother really takes her time deciding what to do between 'Super Black' and a plane to freedom. Because, unlike Michael Jackson, she still wants to keep it 'Super Black'.

Our agent finally shows up in Brisbane Airport. He is a brother, from the motherland. His name is John. He helps us put everything in the car. We start our drive, and halfway through, I notice an enormous billboard. It reads 'Wacol Prisons'. Wacol Prisons? We drive by Arthur Gorrie Correctional Centre, Brisbane Correctional Centre and Brisbane Women's Correctional Centre. I turn to John immediately. 'Where the hell are you taking my family?!' John answers, 'Welcome to Ipswich!'

We pull up to a house in the suburb of Booval in Ipswich. It is a massive house. Five bedrooms, one for each of us. Me, Angel, Jo, Boni and our mother. My father has not made it here with us.

After the long trip it's been, we go straight to bed.

Arriving in Australia without my father is bittersweet. I would not be here if it were not for him, the sacrifices he made. Despite his shortcomings, of which there were many, my father was fearless. Repeatedly crossing lines and borders to ensure our safety.

One of my father's shortcomings was his temper. Outbursts of anger turned into violence. Through my childhood years, it was always a small beating here and there, but there were worse moments. One time I am eleven years old. I need some pocket money to go hang out with some friends. I go into my father's room and open the drawer where I know the money will be. I grab a few notes. Just as I am about to make my escape, I turn around and he is at the door. He got the drop on me.

He says nothing. Just opens his hand and I put the money in it. He points to the floor, and I kneel with my hands behind me, fingers crossed. I am expecting the usual, belt or extension cord. My head is facing down. I am waiting.

Like a strong wind with steel attached to it, the slap on my right cheek throws my balance off, sending me to the corner of the room. I am lying on my back, hands up in defence. He takes one step forward and stops. Our eyes meet. Shame on his face. Fear on mine. He puts the machete down.

In that moment with our eyes locked, we both understood that something had been lost. The ability to really see each other, as a father and son are supposed to.

I wake up that first morning in Ipswich wanting to see my new neighbourhood. I walk out of the door. It's about 10 am. I am wearing a red hoodie, earphones on my head, listening to good music. I walk from the end of our street, where our house is, to the main street, Jacaranda Street.

Walking towards Jacaranda Street, I see nice-looking houses. I notice someone peeking through the window to look at me. More than once, when I look their way, they close the curtains. I shrug it off and enjoy my walk.

I walk past a church and a school, and shortly after I hear the siren sound. I panic and stay calm. I am calm because I know I have done nothing wrong. Yet, deep down, part of me knows they are coming for me. We have seen or heard it before. An armed or unarmed black teenager wearing such-and-such shot dead. I am eighteen years old, I have my life ahead of me, so much I want to do.

The police van pulls over behind me, and I stop walking. Two police come out of the car—a man and a woman. The police officer looks me up and down. He does this without breaking or flinching one moment, while his hand is firm on his weapon. As if to say, I dare you to make a scene.

They shuffle to stand on opposite ends of the pavement, so I am stuck in the middle. The other police officer brings out her notepad. I pause my music but keep my hood on.

The male police officer finally says, 'Where are you going, son?'

I think for a second, son? I am not your son. I answer him, 'I . . . I do not know. I am new here?'

'Is that so? And you don't know where you are?'

I try to stay calm so I can answer his questions.

'Where do you live?' he asks.

'Um . . . around . . . here, bear with me a second, I remember. One second . . . 13 Welsby Street. Have I done something wrong here?'

'No, son, this is just a neighbourhood check. So, your name and your date of birth?'

His partner notes all this down and they get back in their van and drive away. I think to myself, am I the suspect of a crime I have yet to commit? I turn around and walk back to Jacaranda Street. I turn left on Welsby Street and look at that house as I near it. I cannot shake the strong suspicion my neighbours called the cops on me. My first day in Australia. How many escapes does one have to make in life?

As I walk past my neighbour's house, I take a glimpse, see if they are still there. I take my hoodie off. I want them to see me. Head un-bowed and unflinchingly the last person standing. It is the beginning of a new tune. A unique sound altogether. A change of channel and frequency at play here. Because . . . well, when the music changes, so does the dance.

I am paralysed by the ordeal. I don't victimise myself, how can I? Living in Malawi surrounded by other black people, it never occurred to me to consider my black skin, I feel alien in this place. And my appearance has not changed here, with the exception of hair and outfit, the people staring have changed and my teenage mind cannot compute this, what it means. What is blackness in the face of whiteness—inferior? I am experiencing it, and I didn't know that the mode of segregation and discrimination had been set before I got here. I walked home covered in shame of not feeling welcomed. I've felt this before. How am I meant to assimilate and come to terms with this community? The police drove away in pride probably. Pride in their work: dehumanising other in bare nakedness. Leaving me to question what's wrong with me? Du Bois called this feeling double consciousness—duality. A series of characteristics attributed to a group of people. I obviously look black, but the colour does not identify me or define me—I'd hope my experiences do.

Their language has failed us: keeping order. A sort of macho Rambo, a militant body language of protection and service, a police-adopted monologue across the globe, leaving their victims outnumbered in support and ammunition. We are abandoned, the rest of our remaining words being, 'I can't breathe' or 'I am not armed.' Words that came out of David Dungay Jr and George Floyd multiple times before they died. These niggas look just like me. The reality is the words were dead before they left their bodies. They were dead long before they knew it—before they could say . . . empty words. As I write mine here, I wonder about the meaning and value they hold. If I can't even tell you sincerely how I feel. If I cannot explain—how you make me feel under my darker skin. If I cannot say and stay. Then, where do I go from here?

As I walked back to my new home on that day in July 2014 there was a pain in my chest, I fell off the crest. I could have completed my journey, but I didn't even bother, my day was ruined. My future was ruined. And the past I had

come from had been ruined as well. What's left for me?
I think to myself, what is it about me that scares you? Is
it my hood? Skin tone? Or my mother tongue? Whatever
it is, it's not on me. I know what's on me. I see them cross
the street as I walk on the same side as them. I look good,
handsome. I smell good, Tom Ford. I am dressed nicely, in
vogue, and yet I feel the need to be contained, maintained.
Tamed as if in a zoo, as if the streets have warning signs,
the kind you find in the wild. Something that would read,
BEWARE OF BLACK.

Four months later from this incident, in Chicago a
teenager named Laquan McDonald, who was black, was
shot sixteen times by a police officer, who is white. I am
telling you this happened because it was so close to mine.
Colour or creed has nothing to do with crime, but dare
we forget we are black, you are quiet to say, to remind, the
gap created. So much so that the law enforcement crimes
committed hold nothing of substance, colour or otherwise.
No justice, no due process, no nothing.

Everyone is outraged every time something happens,
another unarmed black boy.

I never shared my encounter with the police with my
family, that day or ever. Something terrible happened to
me and I couldn't articulate it to them. I was not equipped
to understand my situation. Also, I had it in my mind,
we had bigger fish to fry. So, life went on and on. I had
hoped you would knock on my door and leave your apathy
outside and listen to this story. I pity the growth of your

apathy and guilt. Pity your pride, your pride in shame. You wouldn't use these words, but like I say, language fails us.

One time in Redfern, I had a conversation with this lady, a mother. A mother of a son. A son she had lost to police brutality. She was in pain. Different pains. 'Black Fella,' she said to me after a show at the Tudor Hotel; 'they took my son,' she said, almost in tears. And then she pointed to her son on the t-shirt she was wearing. I sat down with her. During the show and after, everyone dismissed her as a heckler audience. She had tears in her eyes that wouldn't come out. Unexpressed sorrow of the souls of black folks in Australia. Who would chant her son's name?

Australia was built on discrimination, from slave labour of First Nations people to the White Australia Policy. I come into this nation not knowing this, not understanding the effect of this. But the problem is real and immediate here. We need to change the narrative here and directions of these actions.

More than apathy and pride, my fear is a continual amnesia in people. I fear in the same way some people forget Coca-Cola used to put portions of cocaine in their drinks, people choose to forget that civilised and economic life today has been built on the oppression of others. Either we remember and learn to move forward. Or we forget and ignore, only to crumble into the ground. I echo the words of James Baldwin: 'I can't be a pessimist because I'm alive.'

I, too, share this feeling of optimism. I do believe that what has been created and passed on by people can be reversed by them as well.

Two missionaries ride into a village. Wait, forget that. Two Jehovah's Witnesses enter a comedy club. No, no. Two Mormons walk into a bar. No, wait, two Mormons walk in the door, a house door—my mother's house door in Ipswich. And then they sit down on an L-shaped black leather couch. And that, ladies and gentlemen, is how I become a Mormon.

I wonder how it all happened so quickly, if there was a spell involved or voodoo—an origin of some sort, that propelled me to believe in the ridiculous religion. I am desperate to meet people in any kind of hood when I arrive in Australia, and I am converted to Mormonism rather too swiftly. Then into the priesthood—brotherhood—ghettohood—da hood.

Travis is the hook that catches me, my initiator. He is from Ohio, where the religion of the Church of Jesus Christ of Latter-day Saints blossomed. Travis knows that his calling is here in Ipswich, Queensland. Travis is also miles and miles from home. He, though, is here on a mission: trying to convert a somewhat Christian family. Since its inception, latter-day saints have been dispensed to spread the good word throughout the world as missionaries, and two of their best deployments are sitting on my mother's couch right now.

'Do you believe in the word of Jesus Christ?' Travis asks my mother, posing the question, knowing full well that she does believe. It is written all over her face. The air is thin, the tension is real—they carry themselves seriously. They were here last week, and now they're back again with the aid of an interpreter, me. My mother thought they were Jehovah's Witness, otherwise she would not have let them in the house. In Malawi, we got Jehovah's Witnesses all the time. They used to come to our kiosk and house preaching prosperity gospel, salvation gospel. But Mormons are a class above Jehovah's Witnesses. They bring not only Jesus but Joseph Smith.

In our living room the tension feels spiritual, a presence at a seance. After what seems like way too long a pause, I press my lips together and I answer, 'Yes, we do, we are Christian,' adding, 'Pentecostal,' while making eye contact with my mother for a visual consent, for approval. This seems to please both my mother and the men with badges. We proceed.

Travis is sure that my mother's core belief will not be swayed by this new wave of religion he has just presented to us. Naturally, he turns to me, at this point a teenager with a spirit and soul of a plain dish needing flavour. He knows this and so do I. 'Would you like to come to church at some point?' Travis asks while adjusting his bum on the couch like he just let out a fart. He is casual about the ask.

There are a few things in between to iron out before we get to this moment. Travis fiddles with the badge with his name on it. It sits above his shirt's pocket, tacked inside the pocket. He does so like a soldier adjusting his war medals. But eventually we get here. 'Sure, I can swing by to check it out.' And just like that, I open the portal into a rather supernatural otherness. The Church of Jesus Christ of Latter-day Saints in Brassall, a suburb close to Ipswich, is the branch I attend.

Arriving at the church, this Roman-cathedral-like majestic chapel, I am curiously in awe. I feel I am impressionable, but so is the church, so this could go both ways. I meet Samoans at the church wearing skirts. I think it's cool as fuck watching these fashionable believers welcome me into the priesthood. I visit the church more and more. I attend Sunday class with other youths. We play basketball. We are disciples of the Lord, and no one can or will come between us. Parables and proverbs are shared at Sunday school, and they are always my favourite parts of the scriptures. Joseph Smith is introduced to me as the saviour of the book of Mormon. Inside the church, I notice they have high ceilings. Up and up, it goes to heaven. The acoustics are cinematic and theatrical. There is a pipe organ on the left side of the church. A basketball court with glossy floors attached to the back of the church. A stage that children play and dance on, where they worship and praise him freely. It's a massive complex with various recreational centres within it. It is no wonder what happens next, given the enticing and energetic playground they have presented for me. I perform, yes.

Somewhere in the Brassall branch archives exists footage of me teaching Samoan kids to do some African dances. I get asked to do this, humiliate these kids, and I accept. I want to give as much as I am receiving here. We practise for ages, at least twice a week. And with a few days of rehearsal before showtime, I have a profound vision, it was miraculous the way it came to me. I realised I am teaching robots how to dance. These kids are so stiff. No lubrication on the hips or anywhere at all. One child falls on a two-step move! I say child, but really, they are teenagers. Anyway, one of them falls and I think—I foresee—we are doomed. They are not a great representation of God's best. We are going to be a laughing matter.

The night of the performance, everyone comes out to watch, and they are expecting more than we will give them. They will cry of embarrassment, lose faith in dancing, Jesus, African music and black people in one night. Of course, they will blame the choreographer, but I am merely a conduit—don't hang the messenger.

Sometimes I pray. I kneel and pray to the god I don't believe in anymore. I pray that this embarrassing video will be erased from the archive of the church and the world.

We dance to Afro beats and somehow pull it off. No one got hanged or got their legs broken. Shortly after the dance, the ululations and proud parents, I am ordained within the priesthood by Travis. And shortly after, I am baptised into the church. A process that seems fitting for the path that I am on. Because I am going somewhere with this. I am on this path to go someplace promised to me. To be in touch with a higher power. I will be the best missionary to float this planet or other. They will send me to Mars to convert aliens to our ways and I will do it proudly and do it amazingly. The way within the church, of being close to the scripture, is through practise. I go out with the missionaries. I go door to door and preach the good word, an ancient practice, as a door-to-door salesperson. I am getting too good, too quickly, at following the rules. Maybe this is me, a man of order.

They ask me, 'Would you ever consider becoming a missionary in the church?' I think about it, what it means, and ask them, 'You mean dedicate two years of my life to this and nothing else?' Yes, they say.

We walk back to the car to go into the next neighbourhood to find another brother for the priesthood, another soul to save. I take my time to think about it and recite something I came across once. Almost to remind myself, if not to answer their wondering souls, it goes, 'Those convinced against their will, are of the same opinion still.'

There is a silence when we get in the car. We drive off. I am not built for it. Two years is a long time. Am I allowed to have sex during? Can I call my buddy Patrick and talk shit? Patrick will probably laugh in my face. All these thoughts make me wonder maybe I am not of order, I hesitate too much.

My favourite moments in the church have, one way or another, something to do with dance. We go to different branches of the church for the dances. Congregating with others and meeting different people is nice. I get to dance with beautiful ladies, and I am well on the floor. I am imitating and channelling my father. Rotating from one end to another. The Mormons are musically grown so the tunes are groovy. Thank Jesus Christ of Latter-day Saints for that.

I have, at this stage, seen each corner of the church and experienced it all. I am losing patience. What gives, I think? And then, here it is—baptism of the dead. What? Yes, how odd indeed. I already had mine, but the string of baptism we get asked to take part in a little later, are not for the living, necessarily, they are for the dead. Part of the church and its belief is a ceremony that happens now and then at the main branch of each city or state. There is a list submitted of people who have passed, relatives of church members who died without salvation. They need to be saved while they are waiting in limbo—a processing centre if you will. Enter us, the last stroll of hope for them. We can, if we choose, because we are alive, get baptised for them, the dead—the scums—so they can go to heaven.

Cut to the changing room in the main chapel in Brisbane. Surrounded by cream-white high-ceiling walls decorated with white garments as curtains—the same material we wear for every baptism—I am scared for the first time. I have never taken such a leap into any faith. Doing this is on a volunteer basis, encouraged by everyone who has lost a loved one so they can get baptised for them. With the passing of my father, I enlist him and hope this ritual works. I put on a gown and wait to be called out. They call out the list of people who have passed and someone ushers us to get baptised for them, to walk into the pool of water in the centre of the main branch and dip for the first of many today. This one feels special as it is for my father, such that we shall be reunited in heaven or hell.

I walk into the building in Brisbane city, the one I am going to be working in. Epicentre of everything; this is going to be a good sales job. I wonder how much I would make—not much, it turns out. I have ended up in one of those pyramid schemes. It is a commission-based salary. I have had my share of this type of work. Sales job descriptions are what I apply for. Entry level, no experience required. I think I will be trained, surely—I need training. I am the best and all, but give me a leg up, damn it. I'll be in an office moving products from an office up high in the big city of Brisbane—but I end up in a door-to-door sales position, paid only if I make the company more money first. Since I am a student and broke, I accept a shit offer and take a job at LMC Interactive.

Back before I stopped going to church, I met a guy at the Church of Jesus Christ of Latter-day Saints. There is no story or reason why I divorced myself from Mormon-ism and Christianity all together. I just did not find what I came looking for. My curiosity and pleasure ran its course in the faith and its deities, and so I moved on.

This guy I met, let's call him Samuel because I frankly don't remember his name. He is involved in a health organ-isation that signs up people to protein products. A sales pyramid scheme. He gets paid for bringing me in and I get paid for bringing someone else in. Acquiring and selling protein products for the company YOR Health. Being in this YOR Health, I feel like I am in a mob, only less cool. At the induction meeting, which is held at night in a ware-house an hour's drive from my mother's house in Ipswich, we congregate, all of us. We are here to be pioneers and inventors, think tanks, advisers to ministers of health and other health officials everywhere. Nothing more, nothing less. Turn our scars into gold, pour from the pond of pain and mould a success bowl, contain it all. We exchange self-help book recommendations, with authors ranging from Oprah to Garry Vee, and in a circle of confession share what motivates us to become the next 'next'. After a baring of our souls, we receive the packages containing YOR Health products and we hit the street. Not literally, but a remote home business. We get paid only when we sign up someone for these products, seeing as they are free. Well, I paid for them, and so will the customer once they join. But right now, they are free. All sorted and well-thought-out business plans it would seem, except the fact that truly made a difference between me and Samuel making money or not making money—motivation.

Enter motivation conventions with guest speakers from all walks and life to jolt our voltages. And this is how I meet Greg Plitt.

Greg Plitt and I are chatting about motifs. He finished hyping up a full-house crowd on the Gold Coast at Event Cinemas in Robina. I drove with my mate from Ipswich to see this guy. When we heard that our company boss from YOR was inviting the master motivator himself, I had to come see for myself. I bought my one-hundred-plus-dollars ticket and hit the road. I am sitting at the back of the cinema watching him raising the spirits of everyone freakishly. He is pumped. I can tell he has an endless supply amount of motivation in him. I must learn from him. I must know how he becomes this way. At the end of the conference, my friend and I make our way to him for a couple of Q&A of our own. I am in the middle of a conversation with him now and I am, like, yes—my moment. I'll get answers. And so, I ask, 'How? It's the obvious question—but honestly, though, how do you summon the power?' I am proud of myself for having thought of this earlier while he is on stage channelling that very power through his performance. I ask without caring, of course. Without caring or knowing that he will be killed in three months' time. Yes, three months from now Greg Plitt will be hit by a train while shooting a video on the train tracks.

'What's your name?' he says. And we all watch him in awe.

'Oliver,' I answer faux confidently.

'Okay. Look, it's about knowing who you are,' he says with a genuine conviction and his chest out. He is full of bodily muscles, attracting all sexes. Oh yes. I would fuck him right now. We are at an afterparty, and ladies want to talk to him and more (fuck him). I shuffle to the side with my buddy, giving Greg a little smile. We drive back to Ipswich and the rest has been well written about. You know what happens. On a graceful morning somewhere in America, a man with so much motivation is inspired to shoot a video on the train tracks.

About a year later, I find myself in the office of LMC Interactive selling charities and security. I wonder how I fell for this trap again. I make money for the boss and not much for myself. I am going to TAFE in Queensland because my Malawian school credits are not valid here in Australia. I redo my high-school subjects at TAFE and achieve an equivalent of what I already have. I use the credits to study further and get a job. Now, here I am, a door-to-door salesperson, suburb after suburb in the scorching sun. I am working and someone else is reaping the benefits. Not pretty work either for a black boy in country suburbia Australia. If you think Australians are not ready for black people to be in senior positions at companies or hold seats in parliament, try knocking on their doors asking for money.

A 4 am start is the norm. I am desperate. I am doing this work because I need money. I am a manual labourer, who are always in demand anywhere. After doing a Certificate 3 in logistics in Cleveland in Queensland, I end up here—here being a forklift licence driving centre up in the north of Queensland. It is complimentary with a completion of the Certificate 3, a package deal. I am stoked, and so is my mother. I am finally working a proper job. For the first time since arriving in Australia, this is good. How could it not be? Well, it is boring—I am with people twice my age and they have reached the end of the line. I am way too young to be doing shit like this, and it's not my element. It's boring my mind, straining my body. The only interesting thing that happens here is that I burst a water tank while driving the forklift. My spirit of showmanship. I drive this thing home (baseball metaphor). Water goes everywhere, all eyes are on me—what am I doing with myself? I hop off the machinery and head home (actual place).

And then—I am folding paper. I leave the forklift business behind. I am good with my hands, let me put them to use. I fold magazines. Fold anything that needs folding. This is happening in this warehouse near Wacol, I am the youngest, me and the skinny Asian boy. I wake up way earlier than I care to. It's gruelling, but it beats being in Dzaleka refugee camp. Its beats sleeping on one mattress with my sisters in the freezing cold. It beats being on the run from mobs vandalising, tearing kiosks and houses apart. I fold this paper in this factory. I fold here so I can unfold there. Unfold a future of possibilities. I am focused on being on the moon. Once I am on top, they will see my flag. They will know me, they must—there is no other way out of here. Even if I wanted to go back to where I came from—nigga, I can't afford it yet, I am working on it.

VII

My mother knows that today I change my name. She has known for months now. Yet she does not stop me. I want her to object. To tell me I am about to make a mistake and I will disgrace the family name. She does not. So, I walk out of our house in Ipswich and catch the bus to Brisbane.

I walk into the department of registry for a name change. I pick a service number—5A—and take a seat. Few people are waiting. On my lap is a white A4 envelope that I have been carrying in my sweaty palms from Ipswich. The envelope is looking off-white now.

Sweaty palms because I am nervous. My whole life is in this off-white A4 envelope. They need original documents to process name-change applications. The other reason I am nervous is I am afraid the application will be denied on account of that I will not provide my birth certificate.

I am not hiding one. I have never seen it. While fleeing Rwanda, we leave everything behind.

My mother and Angel do not have their birth certificates either. Jo and Boni, who are born in Malawi, do have theirs. As far as documented refugees go, all I have in this off-white A4 envelope is a resident visa. I am hoping it's enough for a name change. My service number is called, and I walk to the counter and hand in the envelope. I walk to Roma Street Station in Brisbane and catch the bus back to Ipswich.

Rwanda was colonised by Belgium and Germany. Not only did they invade Rwanda, but they also invented it. Imposing their ways of being on my people. The differences between Hutus and Tutsis—all made up. So, I question the cachet of our nomenclature system. Our identities revolve around its validity.

My parents name me at birth. Names in Kinyarwanda, my surname meaning 'grateful'. I change it to Twist when I am nineteen years old. Not the most grateful gesture. Twist is a name people adopted when they moved from their hometown to a new place during the European Victorian era. Arriving in Australia from Malawi, Twist fitted perfectly.

I love to have rectified my name to mean something to me or nothing at all. It's a totally accidental, contingent thing. It's pure luck that any of us have the names we do and look the way we do. If you today become a refugee and fourteen years later you have a restart, would you do it all differently?

Most people assume my parents named me Oliver Twist. They invite the far-fetched idea that my parents, somehow in Rwanda, are reading through the pages of Dickens' 'the parish boy's progress'. Shockingly, page after page of reading, they discover the parallels between the life of Oliver Twist and their recently born child.

My whole family has different last names. Keeping a different last name for all family members is common in certain parts of Africa, including Rwanda. I love this. It means every pillar truly gets to stand on its own.

Cool young people who have engaged with a musical version of Dickens' *Oliver Twist* will often say to me, 'Is that your real name? Wow—that's cool.' They say this with exuberance matched only by the value of the item I am purchasing as they fold it into an eco-friendly bag. I wonder sometimes if they mean it or if they are trying to make me feel better about spending money.

The strangest reaction I have got to date about my name is from a security guard outside a bar in Manly. He says, in a recognisable British accent, even after living in Australia for twenty years by his admission, 'I caught a bit of your performance. Oliver Twist, huh?' I flatly answer, 'That's me.' He responds with an old-fashioned, or rather old-engine wit, 'You must get a lot of ha-has from that?' This must have been rhetorical because somewhere between the question mark and my lips preparing a response, I hear a voice not my own. 'Here is one about Oliver hopping on the tube,' he continues. 'What did the conductor on the tube say to Oliver before he hopped off?' I raise an eyebrow, this delights him. He continues with that confidence I know too well from performing on stage, the confidence of knowing the punchline, the direction the story is going. He says, imitating the conductor, 'Hey, Oliver, sit on this (middle finger) and Twist on it!' He bursts into a laugh, adding, 'And there is more where that came from.' He finishes laughing uncontrollably, like those idiots on reality TV shows. I walk away, never looking back again.

On the 8th of September 2015, a little over a year after arriving in Australia, I pull off an impossible trick. I had been begging Fedele, the owner of the Sit-Down Comedy Club, urging him for my time in the ring, to get up and perform. Fedele has a system for booking acts, coloured groupings are allocated, and we all get set times to call. Upon which his phone will ring hundreds of times because hundreds of comedians in and all around Queensland are trying to get a spot in the ring. After knocking on the door endlessly, my time has come, the 8th of September. It's a two-way audition, with me testing the audience and Fedele testing me. I am not performing at his main joint, Sit-Down Comedy Club, because I have not yet proven myself, shown that I can murder, kill. Instead, I am at one of his offshore venues, usually far away from the city. I must catch public transport and rides to have a chance of getting there on time. I want time at the Sit-Down Comedy Club. I want longer sets. I want the big fight. I am a gladiator.

On the corner of a high street, in the suburb of Kelvin Grove, is a hotel. The New Market Hotel, to be specific, I will do my first show here. On the outside, a light design is motel-looking—neon bright lights—and they are inviting. They don't let you know that there is a comedy show inside. And the posters in the clear glass windows are too small to grab anyone's attention. It is a fact left for the locals. Comedy showcases are run by kidnapping an audience, usually for an hour or more if you are lucky.

I take the train and bus there. It is near the Queensland University of Technology and so is frequented by young students—as good an audience as they come. I walk in through the glass sliding doors, all the way to the bar, past the casino room with smokers and gamblers. Bright lights slowly go away, one by one, in a dramatic sense, as I approach a key light. The spotlight projecting the stage.

Leaving my family house earlier today in Ipswich, I don't tell my mother or my sisters where I am going. Here, before getting on stage, I am poised. None of these people know me right now, but I will show them. I will transport them to a different planet, starting with these stories. Open mic comedy is like bull riding. It could go a thousand ways—most of which end with you facing the floor wondering why you thought this was going to be good. New comics meeting first-time comedy-show-goers is a wild, untamed, free experience of a show. Throw a few beers in the mix, in this wild west, and you have a spectacle. They want the puppet to speak their thoughts, tell it like it is and use humour as its bullet. Kill.

I walk to the green room, which is the entire bar. I remember it all vividly. The cable running from the stage to the bar, crossed under the stool audience members sit on—all the way to the plug of the spotlight. A server steps over the cable holding a tray going to table four, a chicken parmesan, sidestepping over the spotlight cable without needing to look down, not needing glow tape, all too familiar with the setup. The stage is miniature. If I take two steps to the left, I'll land on Ross, the sound guy, and the man to impress if I am to get invited back to perform again. He reports to Fedele about who has gone way past the set time, who alienated the audience. He can be such a snitch.

There is lots to learn from my end to maximise my time. For any showcases outside Sit-Down Comedy Club, I look out for who is going to drop in and do a secret set, and I hang around for dropouts so I can get more stage time. Ross himself, being near comics, aka weirdos, is a bit of a strange guy. He takes a liking to me, and we get talking. He used to be in a rock band. He is punk and cut-throat like I imagine a rock and roller would be. He is very anal about time. I am in the third bracket of the line-up tonight.

I watch one by one as everyone goes to perform. I am making mental notes. I am seeing other comedians' sets, and what's tickling the audience tonight. Young students a little drunk on a Monday night—approach with caution. They don't want to be talked to, probably have had full-on lectures. Of course, by the time break two arrives, we lose some audience members, but I am swinging on. One comic after another, each one trying to out-humour the other and be an audience favourite. I am one step closer, one bell ring closer.

Every comic is in the waiting area, aka the green room, buried in their phones checking their notes, reciting their lines in their head, what to say, as well as comebacks to hecklers. I know this because I am doing a version of this myself. I am sitting on a brown leather couch on the left side of the small stage, behind Ross. I see the comics up there not know what to do with their hands, touching the Sit-Down Comedy Club banner behind them. Some, not having spatial awareness, can't see some people behind the two pillars in the bar not laughing. Out of sight, out of mind. I want to get them all. Kill.

I am brought up to stage by an MC and from the moment I take a step to the rostrum, I feel like I belong here. I go that well that first night. I am on a roll of laughter—my stories are full of surprise, and I am spoon-feeding them the jewels. Ross says something like, 'Impressive set, man'. The audience has been saved by the bell, literally. Ross has a bell by his mixer that he dings a minute out from a comedian's five minutes. I am up there for four minutes total, I had them in the corner, swinging and swinging. Punching until the bell dings.

I am ecstatic. Adrenaline runs through me. It is thrilling to make an audience smile and laugh. A superpower. I slow-motion play it over and over. A feeling of being free—of letting someone, albeit a stranger, into my head. Rapture erupting in my body with a sensation I have never experienced before. This is it. I resolve to myself. This is me.

All the kid said was, 'When did you become black?' It takes everything in me to not smack this little white kid. The question really means, why are you black? I guess it runs in the family, little white one. I am tutoring this kid in mathematics, not social studies, not even English. Which is probably where he lacks most. The balls kids have, he looked like a little Eminem (my frame of references for kids is not huge, forgive me). I am at the University of Queensland doing an arts degree. I get this job to earn extra cash.

The campus at UQ is massive, with basketball courts that I frequent for a chill time. I am finding my way through here, not sure what to do. Back home in Ipswich, my mother has high hopes for me. I finished two TAFE courses to get here, to prove that I did, in fact, graduate secondary school. It feels like a waste to give it up and let it go, so many fees spent already. Comedy is not really picking up since I started last year. I am diversifying my classes. Doing the usual employable courses and creative ones for myself to better my chances when I leave this place.

My mother thinks I am built to be a lawyer. My head is always buried in pages, she says. I don't blame her. I could probably be decent at it. I am the first in my direct family to go to university and the first one to drop out, which is a very low bar to set for a first-born child. My mother's very smart and makes good points. Before the war, she used to teach economics. She ended up using her financial skills to help my father run the kiosks. She can speak Kinyarwanda, Kirundi, French, Swahili, Chichewa and English. Very impressive—it all just means she can curse me out in multiple languages.

My sister Angel goes the furthest. All the way to the University of Queensland, where she graduates in a degree I don't remember. Meanwhile, before I am about to decide what to study—the whole town rallies together at my mother's house. An intervention of a sort. 'This child will be great.' 'Oh, he must be a brilliant lawyer.' 'Brains, you can become anything.' I want to drown it all—they don't know what I want, what I am good at. When I drop out, I feel like I am disappointing all of them, their voices. But I do it anyway. My way.

I am twenty-one when I move to Sydney. I grab the little money I have scraped together, pack two suitcases and leave

Ipswich. Arriving in Sydney, I am terrified of becoming homeless because Sydney is very expensive. But I have a subscription to the *Financial Times*. I would be homeless, but at least I would be informed. It's like when you see a homeless person on the street, and they have a smartphone in their hands. And you have that grin on your face, they are fine.

Navigating Sydney can be tricky because it is a big city, bigger than Ipswich. One time I am walking in an alley at midnight from a show and I see this guy standing under a tree. It's dark and his face is blurry. He is making me nervous. When I am close to him, he asks me one question. With a deep, gripping voice, 'Hey, mate, where you from?' One question. 'Hey, mate, where you from?'

And I've been around long enough to know that midnight in a dark alley with a stranger is not the time to be, like, 'It's funny you should ask that. I am Hutu from Rwanda. Pull up a chair. Let me tell you a story.'

Instead, I am thinking he wants to have a go at me, so I just say, 'I am not from around here,' and then I walk past him. Ten minutes later, it hits me. He asked me that because he thought I was the one who was going to mug him, because of my being black. Isn't that a pain, when you think you are in danger, but you are the danger?

I grew up in a dysfunctional family. If you attack me in an alley, I will square up. But also, this morning for breakfast I had eggs benedict. Before that I was in the shower listening to neo-soul music. I am tough, but mellow.

I find my first apartment in Sydney on flatmates.com.au. I am looking for a cheap place in the central area so I can easily get around to shows. I find a place for one hundred and fifty dollars a week in Surry Hills, and I take it in good faith. I arrive there and it's a two-bedroom apartment with one bathroom and five people. Five people. I am in one bedroom with two other people. Three people in one room.

One guy in my room is Takashi, a Japanese international student. Takashi is a sushi chef, so the room is always smelling like raw fish. Takashi says to me one time out of the blue that having a dog as a pet makes you gay. I can see in his eyes that he believes this to his core.

The other guy in my room is Husan. He is Uzbek. He has been in the room the longest and thinks he can do everything he wants. He eats in the room all day. The room smells even worse. He is always having, like, five people over and all they do is drink and eat. Five people doesn't feel like a lot but when you are standing in line in your own apartment waiting to access the one bathroom, five is a lot.

The other bedroom has a couple. They are also from Uzbekistan, which is how they know Husan. They have a baby. The baby doesn't go to school and cries all the time. I don't have a job, so I am in the apartment the whole time praying to God to make me deaf and blind.

As if this is not enough, the genuine pain in my arse is my neighbour downstairs, Michael. He is tall, bald and with a proper beer gut. He sits around all day smoking Winfield Reds. I imagine he has been in the army: he limps when he walks and uses a staff to get around. He is always wearing camouflage shorts. Uses military time in conversation. He says to me one time in a commanding voice, 'Oliver, I went to bed at twenty-three hundred hours last night,' and I am like, 'What the hell are you talking about, Michael? You can't force me to join the army and speak your army language.'

One afternoon, I walk into the apartment complex and guess who is sitting outside. He sees me, his face lights up. As I walk towards him the excitement on his face grows. He puts out his cigarette and leans forward from his hammock chair. I say to myself, 'Here we go.'

He says, 'Oliver, my wife reminded me last night after I talked to you, that you are Rwandisian.'

I say, 'Rwandan.'

He says, 'Yes, Rwandisian.'

Again, I say, 'Rwandan.'

He says, 'Yes, that's what I said. Anyway, Oliver, I'm sorry. I am so sorry. I am sorry. What an awful thing. I'm sorry.'

He said sorry so many times that I said, 'It's okay, Michael—'

'But OH, I AM REALLY SORRY, Oliver.'

Now at this point in the story I am not sure what he is apologising for. Did he take my mail by accident? Did he run over a dog? I don't know. And then I realise, I have been here before, having this conversation. He is apologising for the Rwandan genocide. I ask him, 'Are you Belgian or German?'

He answers, 'No, I am not.'

I go, 'Really? Too bad, because I would love to accept your apology, but I am only taking apologies from white Belgians or Germans right now. You must wait in line.'

He tells me he is Australian. I say to Michael, 'You are a white man in Australia. I think you have misplaced your apology.'

It has been a while since I've moved to Sydney and I am living with a friend, Wolfie. I thought he was a child born and raised in a retirement village and that a couple of grannies with the last ounce of life and time raised him weird. I always found him quirky and out of the ordinary with his day-to-day variety of humour. Baker by day and comedian by night, I had bumped into him first in Redfern at a gig. At the time I was living, rather unglamorously, with no job, in that small flat in Surry Hills. He had just bought a van and started living in it, vacating his attic room in a Waterloo apartment. He lets me move in and for the first time I find breathing room since moving to Sydney.

Here I am in my apartment. I open my laptop and start browsing the web for a meditation centre, wanting to book a reclusive retreat. I've suddenly remembered a woman called Jane with a high-pitched British accent. The accent that, when you hear it, gives the impression that you are listen-ing to something important. Two years before my move to

Sydney, Jane told me she had just finished a silent meditation retreat on the coast of Queensland that changed her life. Hearing this makes me chuckle a little, seeing as she had ended up at YMCA just as I had, mentoring spoilt kids who refuse to focus while in class. I think it didn't change her life that much.

Jane tells me about this meditation practice from Asia. The gist of it is focusing on Buddha's teaching of meditation—aiming to arrive at a peace-of-mind juncture. You pay attention to your sensations with a goal of enlightenment, or close enough. A slow energy always moves around you and within you. Accessing this kind of energy through vibrations, meditating on it, much as the enlightened one does. To open this portal of universal energy, a spiritual grounding is needed, no distractions. You leave your phone, books, magazines, smokes and/or drinks behind—at reception when you arrive at the centre. I am intrigued, thinking surely Mormonism was worse. Jane tells me, 'You can do three, ten or even forty days at the retreat.' I'm thinking, that's great, it is better than signing up to be a Mormon missionary for two years. Since I was a child I've always had a sage energy in me, so I wanted to do this.

I take the mountains line train to reach the meditation centre. Nature engulfs me. An express way to Zen land. Arriving at the centre, on this vast land that's sitting on the top edge of the hills overlooking the mountains, I recall thinking, I am going to die here in the wilderness. But I have survived worse, so I am up to the challenge.

I arrive in the late afternoon along with lots of other people. Some teenagers are getting dropped off by their hippy mothers. I walk to the reception with everyone. At the entrance I meet Jimmy for the first time, a white Australian man. Of course, an Asian traditional practice has been hijacked by a white man.

Jimmy carries himself as a Zen master who is dressed like a modern-day hipster. It's profanity to my ears and a re-education of my eyes. It throws me off so much, meeting Jimmy, I fake laugh. He is wearing cheap loafers, rolled-up khaki pants, and a brown knitted poncho. He speaks with conviction and vigour, with his hands held together in a manner that says, 'I contain a lot of wisdom.' He gives us formalities and maps out a tour of the centre. He does this like delivering a master class. I look at this cult of people collected here and dread the fact that I've signed up for it. Spending time with these strangers. A lot could go wrong.

We meditate for a few hours before going to our designated sleeping places, then get up at 4 am—a starting time for the rest of the days. I am slightly sleepy, but the mountains dawn, coupled with bird noises, keep me awake. Inside the meditation hall, I look around, acknowledging the full room. I lay my blanket first, then the pillow, and then two bolsters lie side to side to support my knees. I am not used to the lotus position. I need the support. I sit down at first without crossing my legs. Focusing on getting into the zone. Jimmy is standing at the door, a smile on his face, applauding our undertaking. I nod at him and pick

143

up my blanket and pillow. I grab a bolster for my knees. I am sitting in the same position as yesterday—the name tag reads 'Oliver Twist'.

It's the second day of my ten-day retreat and a short mystical-looking older man comes in only for the afternoon and night sessions. In the morning, we are on our own. Lucky bugger doesn't have to wake up at four in the morning. The meditation hall is cut in half, men section and women section. It's forbidden to hang out together. We are encouraged to avoid any sexual and other temptations all together.

I open my eyes to take a break after what seems like an hour. We are encouraged to take breaks during the sessions, as they are long. The hall is at full capacity, and silent. I look at the clock. It's five in the morning, time has never moved slower. Damn it, my thoughts are erratic. They are going places. *Light-year is fast. Japan train is fast. Bullet is quite fast too. Okay—come back to earth, this room. Focus, Oliver.* I am near the fire-exit door because seat allocation is alphabetically by surname. If someone transforms into a zombie, I am the first person out of here—I did not pay for this experience. Come to think of it, I did not pay at all. So, I am truly free, in my actions and contributions. I close my eyes and get back to it—I am easing into it now. Complete concentration: an hour passes and the bell rings. It's breakfast time.

I am sitting on a thick unpolished wooden bench on the balcony, watching the mountains come to life. The sun beams on us on the balcony, filling us with much-needed vacation beams. Giving all nature surrounding us life. I am having a delicious smooth porridge for breakfast—it settles in nicely. I have not had porridge since I left Malawi, and I am feeling nostalgic. There are two main options for breakfast: porridge and toast. No toast as it's too crunchy and my teeth are sensitive.

On the balcony here, I am contained with serenity watching the sunrise from the mountains with the spring clouds clearing as the fog disappears, sipping a mug of green tea held in my two hands carefully, like a new-born. Visible breaths come out of my mouth like smoke. My bowl of porridge, now empty, is on my left, below the timber bench. I look up from the last sip of my mug and I see Louis standing facing me, leaning his back on the edge of the balcony. His sudden presence startles me, he just appears like a creepy ghost, sidles near me—I can never see him coming. Right now, he is nameless. I will get to know his name at the end of the retreat when we talk. He is wearing a blue jacket and gloves, wool on the inside of his jacket, he is about six feet tall with short grizzly hair and a beard that has not been washed for at least two years. He smiles and nods at me, his face suggesting he is searching for something, and I will hear all about it on day ten. I head inside to return the mug and bowl. I head back to the temple to continue meditating.

Leading up to the course, they forbid any intake of drugs. The reason being that we are going to aim to reach that ecstatic state naturally. It is day four here at the centre. I am feeling wildly joyful, not the same as taking ecstasy or mushrooms, but close. My stress is eased and there is no pain, physical or emotional. The amount of comfort I get from meditating in these woods is liberating and healing. I could stay here forever. The world outside me is un-desirable. I want nothing else.

The first time smoking cannabis for me is in Malawi. My parents were right that I was smoking, just not with whom they thought, the gang or the mob. I start with a group of friends I know around town where we were living in Chilinde, Lilongwe. Not too much because my tolerance is low. It's very relaxing for me and everyone around me partaking. It's a different type of relaxation compared to meditation. It did cross my mind that the ultimate relax-ation would be smoke and meditating. But then the other part of my mind that has not been affected by the smoke thinks, no—I would just fall asleep, which is peace of mind: relaxation. Recreationally, I have done only a handful of drugs. While they differ from person to person, experience to experience, eliciting different feelings and energy, for me they are not a replacement for a natural state of peace, and this is clearer while I am here. The chase only takes you so far. Soon you must confront issues sober.

I thought silence was the absence of sound, but after five days of being here, I realise silence is the absence of familiar sounds and I miss them all. The familiar sounds. I miss the sound of rain when it hits my balcony back in central Sydney. It never rains heavily here in Australia, not like back home in Rwanda. This measurable rain is giving my succulent plants on my balcony a perfect dose of water, I imagine. I miss the sound of my sisters and my mother laughing. I miss the sound of the plane taking off from the tarmac in Malawi when we came to Australia. I miss the sound of the city that knows no silence or solitude, the busy big city—the energy flowing through everyone, a kind of rush hour to get home, the beeps, trains, birds and drilling sounds of a city always under construction. I miss the sound of the call to prayer by the mosque in the Dzaleka refugee camp. I miss the sound of the preacher reassuring me, as a child, that I am safely protected by the creator of the universe, his voice, and that of everyone in the church. I miss the sound of vuvuzela trumpeting in our Pentecostal church when I blow into it during praise and worship.

I miss home. I miss the sound of home. The waterfalls, the rooster waking me up in the morning. Late-night sounds of house parties. I miss the sound of the skipping rope on the playground in Dar es Salaam in Tanzania with friends. I miss the sound of music when I am high.

I miss the sound of banter at bars and cafés. I miss the sound of tension in cinemas and theatres. I miss the sound of the audience laughing when I am on stage. I miss the sound of them chatting as they wait for the show to start.

But I do not suffer from selective hearing. I don't miss the sound of the random girl crying and threatening to kill herself in my living room because she is having a bad acid trip. I don't miss the sounds of the gunshots I hear while my mother is folding clothes in Dar es Salaam. I don't miss the sound of soldiers breaking into our house in Malawi, screaming for us to leave. I don't miss the sound of soldiers shooting during a riot in Malawi, or when Donald's wicked witch is caught. I don't miss the bullet shells hitting the rooftop of our house in Malawi. I don't miss the sound of the sirens of the police car that came after me on my first day in Australia. I don't miss the sound of sirens, period, because it stresses me out.

I don't miss the sound of my mother crying from my father beating her. I don't miss the sound of myself crying from him beating me. I don't miss calling out Boni's name or Jo's name in the streets when they go missing in Malawi. I don't miss the sound of my father's name being called by the village chief's second-hand man announcing his funeral.

Moses is homeless, he comes here to the centre not only to meditate but for the shelter, food, and every amenity the centre offers. The rumour is that he lives under a cave in the city. Moses is here with me hand-washing our pile of clothes. Well, looking back, I guess he came here with his entire house, a true nomad. I call him Moses because he has a beard. He doesn't emulate or uphold the rules of the centre. He leaves the centre whenever he wants, which is boss. The whole time I have been here, I have seen him leave the centre multiple times and only caught his view a handful of times in the temple. He has been here before. It is halfway between me squeezing the last ounce of water in a shirt and grabbing another item to wash when Moses opens his mouth, to break the vow of silence, and starts speaking.

My ears know he is saying something to me. I am looking in my bucket, washing my underwear with the midday heat from the sun hitting the hanging clothes. He is not here, he is not talking to me. I am halfway through the course already. I am not about to throw it all away. Out of sight, out of mind. Moses smiles at me in his gown while washing socks, a sinister smile. He laughs and I look up at him and he is still laughing. I want in on the joke. Moses keeps laughing in my direction and I am waiting for the joke to hit me, but he is holding back, and the suspense is killing me. His look suggests that there is only one way to find out what the fuss is all about.

I go up to the ropes to hang my underwear, and Moses goes, 'Do you want to see something interesting?' and I give him the face that says, 'About time.' He looks around to see if anyone is looking. He then gestures for me to follow him. We go behind the bathroom. Looking at what Moses is precisely laughing at, I think to myself, wow! There is Jimmy with his pants down, showing his naked butt, having sex with a woman. I look at Moses with my best Gen-Z opportunistic face, as if to say, 'This is good content.' We duck behind a rock and Jimmy keeps checking behind his shoulder to see if anyone is looking. Moses says, 'Cheeky bastard is going around enforcing celibacy and this is how he gets down.'

Moses and I get back to washing our clothes, leaving Jimmy to his business.

Day ten, I am in the kitchen and it's six in the evening. It's not dinner, lunch or breakfast—a last gathering. I left the temple—mediation hall—ten minutes ago for the last time in all its majestic glory, quietness and loudness. I will miss it dearly. We had come to an understanding, the temple and I, when I arrived here, that it will indulge my erratic thoughts and my feelings. I will honour its stillness. In the last hour, Jimmy comes to the front of the centre. I give him a look of 'I know how you get down, mate'. He breaks the silence code by thanking everyone around us and telling us tomorrow morning we get our belongings back and go home. 'Remember,' he says, 'practice is the way.' Jimmy joins a group to mingle and chat. We are set loose to talk to each other.

Slowly, like a stadium wave or chant, the chatter is spreading through the room, picking up momentum from person to person. We are all sitting on tables like in the last supper painting. Louis goes first. 'There is a cult café not far away. We should stop by tomorrow on our way home.' Everyone lets out a laugh that quickly dwindles when we realise by his expression that he is not joking. At this stage, I am on my second cup of the best natural chai I have ever had. My eyes are wide awake, listening to Louis tell us about the cult café. He is going on and on about it. We all agree maybe we should pay it a visit. We did not.

Louis knows a lot about cults, it turns out. Apparently, across the road is a cult church where his ex-partner is going. The way he made that transition, I cannot remember. At this stage, I regret Jimmy permitting everyone to talk. I face the other two people and start chatting away. They seem normal to an extent and small talk eventually runs its course. I turn back and Louis has taken a tangent of explaining that 'Aliens are here on planet earth' and that they have been feeding on gold since their arrival. All this he says while everyone is exchanging funny looks. 'There are only a few of them here on earth because they left to go find gold elsewhere since we have run out.' I laugh in disbelief. Louis, offended by this, says he has proof. One piece of proof is a conference video he attended where they had gold, half-bitten by the aliens. 'You could touch the gold and feel the vibrations, sensations, if you will,' Louis says. My cynical mind keeps posing questions to Louis that create more holes in his story, and he says he will grab my email and send me all the proof. We all nod to end this conversation and scatter like exposed cockroaches. Five years later, and I am still waiting for that email from him.

VIII

MY FIRST TIME IN THERAPY is with Jonah's mother. I get a bus, train and then another bus to her house, which is at least an hour from where I live. She lives in Rose Bay, and I have only known one other person who lives in the Eastern Suburbs. When the second bus stops, it's a short walk to her house. I enter through the back door and in the kitchen is a man who I think is her retired husband. An older man with a grey beard wearing a coat as if he is always cold. He would be Jonah's father. I watch him sit on the kitchen stool while she prepares tea for me. I always ask for tea—there is something nice about tea in therapy that makes me 'open up' even more. A goal of mine in coming here is to be more open. I mean, if you had the pleasure of meeting me, you would know how lively I like conversations to be—open for business twenty-four hours. These magical moments are all thanks to therapy.

She is fond of me, and opens with, 'How are you doing this week?' To which I answer, 'I am doing okay.' I have been raised by a family in an environment that demanded so much from me. I grew up too soon. I remember times where I would be lectured either by our preacher or teacher that this is the way it should be, about how hard things are, and that it will be that way, so we'd better get used to it. Now here, hearing Jonah's mother say to me in her own way, telling me, I should stop being too hard on myself. My heart sinks. I mourn my innocence—my eyes' purity, the things I see. The things I saw weigh on my young conscious even still. I am trying, I tell Jonah's mother.

She was recommended to me by my GP, who I approached, telling him, 'I need to talk to someone. I remember horrors from home.' I am being tormented by them. I can't sleep sometimes and when I do, I am having nightmares. I just cannot keep this to myself anymore, going like before. I need to heal and reveal these feelings— my sensibilities.

A genocide exile is the phrasing he used, my GP, while writing a referral letter. It always sounds extreme, when put in those words. 'That's intense stuff for a young man,' he says with a tinge of empathy. It is strange to think of the kids only after the fact. During the conflict, no one stops to think about it at all, not for a second less or more. To think of what's happening to a generation of kids to come. I accept his letter, a chance to remedy my past, and patch things up for my clarity, my sanity.

I tell Jonah's mother my goals for coming to see her. She starts with a basic recommendation of jotting down my emotions on a piece of paper. How I feel. And scoring those feelings. To make me think about the degrees of my feelings. I am kept awake with night terrors. I tell her of riots in Malawi and domestic violence at home that traumatised me as a child. One root of my issues is that my dead father tormented me and my family. I tell her this, not expecting much. It's not fair to ask too much of the dead, after all—there is no use even. But I will try it.

My father once said to me, 'If I had five kids like you, Oliver, I would jump into a river full of crocodiles.' What a thing to say to your only and first-born son. This kind of rhetoric mostly defined how I remember this man. Snippets of conversations that weren't so nice. If I said that to someone today, let alone my son, I would have to jump into a river full of crocodiles afterwards myself. What a phrase, though, huh? Crocodile Dundee couldn't come up with a sharp line like that.

A recurring dream I keep having that has me end up here, in the sinking chair in Rose Bay by the water-view cliff, involves my father. The dream, rather a nightmare, is of my father coming into my room in my apartment in Waterloo. This alone is a scary thing for a younger me; my father always scared the shit out of me. A man raised in a country on the brink of genocide since birth, of course crocodile-river-jumping has crossed his mind. He slept with a machete by his bed like a nineteenth-century

Japanese ninja, always on alert. In the dream, my father kicks down the front door like it's a drug-bust operation. I wake up in my attic room two levels up and start rushing downstairs, all the while watching my head so as to not bump it on the low ceiling of the attic. I get down to the living-room area. No one is here, not my housemates, just me alone, with a barrel of water sitting by the wide-open door. He appears suddenly to kick down the barrel and water pours out of it. I am terrified of drowning—always have been. This dream brings two fears to the surface. My father and rising water, and there I am. Not moving like a shadow, a photo of a shadow, paralysed. I am panicking in my dream, and reality. A state of sleep paralysis. I wake up panting. Rinse, repeat, every few months. Same thing: panic kicks in and out. I tell my therapist about this after stalling with financial stress and relationship trouble, a misdirection.

She asks me to think of a moment that my father exerted power over me. It's easy to find a time but hard to go down that memory lane. Sympathy for the devil is what we are about to engage in—we dissect no one else but him, we understand no one else but him. This part of therapy I don't like. She suggests a process, Eye Movement Desensitisation and Reprocessing (EMDR), being well versed in it, her specialty for treating trauma. It's a therapy technique designed in the eighties. She must get my verbal and written approval for us to engage in it. I agree and off we go.

I am about eleven years old, and my father comes home one night, angry. I don't know why. He comes from the kiosk. We live in an open-space studio, warehouse-style. I can hear his angry attitude through his voice. He is flipping tables, and it wakes me up. I can see through the green mosquito net he is holding my mother by the head, grabbing her hair, dragging her across the room to the other side of the house. She has one hand on her braids on the skull to stop the pain and the other on the floor to stop the movements. She is crying, making me cry as well. He is screaming, 'Where is the money?!' Again, he repeats, 'Where is the money, Josephine?!' She doesn't answer, and he whips her with the belt. I know how that feels. It pains me, make it stop. He doesn't stop. He beats her, flipping their mattress over. Angel wakes up. At this point in the story, Jonah's mother is looking at me, conflicted. Professionally, she wants me to go further, but personally, she needs me to stop. My hands are shaking like I have been bouldering for too long and too fast. I can feel the nerves on my fingertips—my skin pulsing. I continue the story. I need to let it out.

I cover Angel's ears, so she doesn't hear our mother sobbing. Is he drunk? I think not. He is sober, even worse somehow in my mind—in everyone's mind, the police's mind? Someone call the police. Anyone? He has issues though. He is fucking awful. Sympathy for the devil? Never. I hate him for this—I always will. Shit! Back to the scene again, this time going further, she says, 'Stop whenever.'

Last time I stopped at me hearing him angry before he beats her, stopping just before I get useless. Hopeless, paralysed by fear. Motionless.

I am trying to wipe off my tears, but I can't—in my hands are these bars she has given me for body monitoring. She asks me on a scale of one to ten what I am feeling and to rate it, give it a number, based on this event—1 being okay with it, 0 at peace with it and 10 fucking triggering. I say ten. It's scary and frustrating that I can't do anything. When I wake, she says that's okay. The point of this is to go over and over the traumatic experience until it's less so. We do it again then, and again until tears are on my cheeks, dropping to my thighs and I sink further into the couch. The room is non-existent because I have been transformed, transported to where it's all happening.

Angel cries in the memory, a detail I never reached in other sessions. And it breaks my heart. Seeing our mother like this, helpless and brutalised by our father. Then we stay there until we go back to sleep of our own volition. I remember the next day clearly, too. My therapist never asked about this day, though. The next day—my mother's friend from church is there. I guess my mother calls her. My father is nowhere near the house.

I get ready to go to school, my mother aiding me to. And I listen to her—eavesdropping. Angel stays at home this day. I look at my mother's face, all swollen in parts, listen to her talk to her friend. She says, 'I have the money and I want to leave him.' And that's it. Her friend says nothing, and neither does she again. I leave the house to go to school. In class I am daydreaming. Imagining my mother leaving with my sister to go home to Rwanda and leaving me with him. This shouldn't happen. I can't allow this. I am not staying back with him. I run out of the class, running home all the way. I am praying to God that she is there.

I am catching my breath as I approach the gate. I have never run so fast. I go inside and I run into my mother's arms and burst into tears. 'Please don't leave me with him, take me with you.' She consoles me and we stay here, and then she nuzzles me forward, so she can look at my face. 'I would never leave you,' she says. And I am now safe, maybe even at peace, at least for now.

Back in that session with my therapist, she asks me, 'What would your older self now have done in that situation?' And I give her a reasonable answer: 'I would stop him and call the cops or get help.' But looking back now, I wish I'd told her my true feelings. Now that I am a man, I would walk over to him myself and push him over the cliff into a river full of crocodiles.

Jonah's mother is my first therapist after moving to Sydney. My second therapist is a holistic lady that comes recommended by a colleague of mine. I know I won't see her for long after our first session. I don't mean to paint a parkour-like patient picture of myself, who hops from doctor to doctor. I am not picky at all. Jonah's mother is expensive, and holistic lady, not so much. One reason I see her.

My first session with holistic lady goes well enough. I walk to a waiting area that looks like a living room. It's massive and small at the same time. Nordic and traditional—holistic lady is of Indian background. There are a few statues around of various gods she is fond of. It's a clinic and yet it doesn't feel like it. There is a reception without a receptionist, ever. It's in Bondi, a rightful place for a holistic centre. Everyone in Bondi believes in self-improvement. It's a religion. She always has clients waiting. The bell rings and that's when you know your time is over. More than once, our session is cut off by someone ringing that damn bell.

I am here because she is cheap, and my story is not finished. I need to tell it in full. Therapists, unless they know each other, don't really pass notes, I don't think. So, it feels weird to tell different parts of your life to a string of people. You tell the painful stories repeatedly, but then, if you are doing therapy right, it gets better as you go. You are free to tell the truth. She has a mat on the floor. In two weeks, I will lie on this mat, and I will feel just like I imagined, which is this feels too familiar, too much like being in the camp, being poor. Ground-floor experience for most things is not for me, let alone therapy. If I am to expose my soul, at least let me be comfy.

We go through what I like to call my second-degree burns with the holistic lady. I had left Jonah's mother feeling well looked after and having dealt with a part of me that troubled me for years of my life. Holistic lady and I start with relationships, of which she says she has been through herself—I am thrilled for her. I am telling her my dilemma of wanting a long-lasting relationship but touring and other work commitments making it difficult. I tell her of feeling inadequate and being behind on my planned career trajectory. She tells me to 'watch what you eat' because it affects how I feel about things now, which is true, I guess. Also, a very Bondi phrase.

I have never been to a group therapy session, but this holistic lady conducts our one-on-one sessions as if they are group ones. Pausing longer, as if someone else is going next. The day she lays me down, she says, 'Imagine these people here and there,' gesturing at positions in the room. Imagining people in the same room while I lie on the floor makes me feel like I am in a zoo, or this is an intervention—not helpful. I don't like it. She recommends I read *The Body Keeps the Score*. I get a copy, but every time I sit down to read it, I can never get past a few pages. Maybe I will try getting a mat, lying down and see if I can go through it this way.

Jonah is my third therapist. Our first sessions are in a smoky room, a haze to be specific, brought about by me. I am still smoking cigarettes when I see him. In a hazy room like a backstage of a theatre, he lets me puff my way through our sessions. I didn't know if I was going to pick up where his mother and I left off. It's not like she is dead, and the family members have taken over like a family-run drug-cartel therapy clinic. No, not at all. I get a phone call from Jonah's mother a few months before I see Jonah. She checks in with how I am going. After the formalities are out of the way, she tells me that her son is soon to graduate from university and become a psychiatrist. He needs a therapy case to graduate, and she thinks I am perfect for it. She sets up a call for me and her son.

I am in Melbourne at the Retropolis vintage store when I get a call from Jonah. He is relatively young by the sounds of it, his voice is soft. 'I got your number from my mother,' he says, laughing a little through the awkwardness of it. He must have heard I am a comedian. I walk through the clothing section of Retropolis, browsing colours, layers that match and go well with my skin tone. We discuss what he is proposing, an intensive two-days-per-week agreement of talk therapy. I see a teal jacket and consider it.

I come back from Melbourne to Sydney. First on the schedule, my sessions with Jonah—who in person looks not the way he sounds. I come through the reception in a medical centre in Summer Hill. He has set up an office on level two. He takes a seat further into the room and I sit close to the door. The office is minimal. He asks me if he can record our session and I say all right. He has a delight-ful laugh, the kind that is sincere and encouraging. If my sessions with Jonah's mother were aiming at root core issues with my father, Jonah will continue right from there, like an orchestra passing the melody from one section to another. I tell Jonah about my mother and off we go with parent number two.

My mother, I should say, much like nineties gangster rappers, is of a high belief that therapy is snitching. To this day, she doesn't know I am in therapy. My mother's attitude towards not being vulnerable is the same reason I am in therapy. In this similar stream of thinking, my mother could not be Catholic at all. The idea of confession is hell for her.

Jonah is understanding, always asking about my sisters and how they are coping. I deeply care about them. As I was leaving Ipswich, my mother lamented that I was abandoning them, leaving her, saying she was thankful that her daughters were by her side. When I went back in those earlier times to celebrate their citizenships, Jo was in tears and Angel had become my mother in all ways possible.

My mother is one of seven children, and only one of them was a boy. When the Rwandan genocide started, she fled with my father to Congo and some of her relatives were killed during the unrest, including her brother. She doesn't talk about it. Every visit home I feel like I am fishing for the missing puzzle pieces, something to hold water, something to take me back to where it all started, my mother tongue, my mother country. My breakthrough moment in therapy is when I find out how to carry myself, not as a victim of genocide in exile, but as a lucky human being—one to experience a wonderful gift. The household I grew up in as a child was built on nerves, sweat and fear. I want a house built on the opposite, to take care of my loved ones. And this, I find, is a daily uphill battle.

After the Rwandan genocide, everyone in my household decided to not revisit the past. Rwanda is in the past, and so is my father. I'd like to unfold the envelope to see what is buried inside. I want to walk down the street and belong; I long for a kind of joy, and yearn to be seen as clearly as the streets I walk on. If I am to imagine a future for me and a family, the pillars and foundations of the house are these which are true, and which are clear from the burden of tiptoeing around landmines of family history and unexpressed emotions.

Boni, my youngest sister, is in a way the only one who's had therapy. Physio and speech, her disability is such that she needs it regularly. Boni's birth met my parents at a hopeless time. Everything we had tried to get out of Malawi and out of the Dzaleka refugee camp had failed. They lost hope and Boni's condition did make it worse, the feeling of being stuck. My mother goes out of her way not to bring it up. She was in denial for a long time. My father, too. They would say things would get better, Boni would get better, she wouldn't have to live like this all her life. But our nature was that we were poor refugees, and Boni's nature is hard for us to accept. She will not have a simple life, but we are here, together, for her.

IX

I HOP ON A TRAIN from Sydney to Newcastle in New South Wales, to see my dear good friend Rowan. He moved back up to be closer to his family and try to make it work with his girlfriend, who lives out here. As far as healthy examples of someone who is living without spiralling—he is at the top of my list. I have one duffle bag with me for a week-end-long stay. I am staying at his family's house in one of their spare rooms.

Rowan picks me up at the station, and we drive all the way to his house. He is a big huggable Sri Lankan man. Our greetings affirm this. In the car I want to hear everything about him and Isabel. We pull up to his house in Newcastle. It's my first time at his house. The doors look like the Pearly Gates. I believe there is a bible in the foundation of this house—a story for him to tell you sometime, just pay him a visit or ring him. Look him up.

Newcastle is one of those places that has a weird air around it. It has the biggest McDonald's, or KFC, built here on Aboriginal graveyards—a disgrace. During and after its construction, it stirred controversy a few years back. I walk past the cafés, past the surf kiosks, past the record store and this McDonald's or KFC. (Is it maybe a Hungry Jack's? No, it cannot be, they don't have that kind of money.) I walk all the way to the bridge near the beach. I am taking a tour that brother Rowan has blessed me with. His mother is a professor and his father a doctor, he is a unique brand of creative, and has that rebellious streak that makes him a close friend of mine. At a young age, he would make his parents drop him on streets so he could busk. Yes, he is built different.

At the house his mother welcomes me as her son, through excess home-cooked meals. I am only here for a couple of days, enough to see a loving dynamic nuclear family that talks and eats together at the same table. I love him dearly, and every time I see him, I ask about his family. Rowan and I talk about building families, a home. As older siblings in our families, we feel a tremendous responsibility to be a symbol for how to get it done.

He beats me to it, gets a head start. Rowan gets married to the lovely Isabel, and I am back in Newcastle for the wedding. I am so thrilled for him and his wife. I admire his tenacious behaviour—taking forward steps and making choices that inspire me. He asked me and Aleks to host his wedding and it was a wonderful time. A celebration I was happy to be part of. It is a great joy to see him so thrilled. I hope to absorb as much of that by being around him.

Mother's Day in my mid-twenties. I am helping my mother move house. Moving is a strong word for what this is. She and my sisters have been given notice that the house they are living in is being sold—the house I lived in first in Ipswich, Queensland. Ash Barty, of tennis fame, is from Ipswich—she is why my mother lives in Ipswich. That's a lie, but it is the way I choose to look at it. It makes Ipswich sound more interesting. Otherwise, there's not much there and, frankly, I do not see why she stills lives there.

My mother has asked me to move all their belongings into storage. I am mad at her for letting things get this bad. She is allergic to change of any kind. My sister Angel picks me up from the airport. I always dread coming back here unless it's for work. Ipswich, Queensland, bores me. My mother has resorted to living in a motel with Jo and Bo because there is no house in Ipswich close enough to Boni's school for students with disability needs.

My mother is in the kitchen cooking. We loved watching cooking shows together when I lived with her. An instinctual cook too, recipes are for creepy families (no one cares about your grandma's creepy family recipe, Janet). Our family is not creepy, just dysfunctional. I am in the living room flicking through photos of the family. My mother has lately removed my father's photos from the album. I flick through our photo collection, seeing some faces I don't recognise. I ask her who they are and why I have never heard of them. A moment freezes. She looks at me and tells me a fresh smell of a secret. Which is that Seba is not my father's name.

My father—I have known him as Seba. I have known this my whole life. I recall moments before interviews for resettlement in the early 2000s in Malawi, right outside UNHCR offices. He kneels. 'Now, Olivier, when they ask your father's name you say 'Seba'. And when they ask you who you are, you say 'Hutu'. Okay?' I nod in agreement. Once inside, they ask me as he said they would, and I repeat his answers verbatim. The man behind the desk shuffles our answers and the ruffle of our futures is underway.

'What do you mean Seba is not his name?' I protest, but she pays me no mind. She says it is his friend's refugee status paper that my father had. Our status didn't get approved, so he used his friend's, a Congolese man, for our application to Canada. She has a superpower, my mother, of making up alternative stories, alternative realities all together. How do you go on pretending you are someone else? A true fabricator, a creative, a storyteller. A story goes: arriving in Malawi in 2000, my father agreed to a deal with his friend Seba. Seba is to go back to Congo, and we inherit, at a price I am sure, his status and thus identity. This allows my father to establish himself with a place to stay in the camp.

My mother casually shares this with me while sizzling some onions. They smell so nice. What's in them? Just onions? I want to devour every morsel of that soup or salad, whatever she makes them with. Emmanuel is the name given to my father, she says. Also, my middle name and my mother's brother's name. All within us, God's with us. Emmanuel is a wonderful name. This lie tells the truth of the situation of the unknown, the invisible, the displaced. The optional. You too could be one of us, pick a war, any war. Join us now and spend little or more money, depending on how the war treats you, investigating your family, forever, your identity endlessly skewed.

I am sitting on a black half-circle couch. Wondering if I ever knew my father at all. But, boy, does it smell good in the kitchen. I almost forget I am mad. I take my Mother's Day gift. Wrap it up. Just like everything else in the house. A box of mystery. Tomorrow, we have a removalist coming to help us put things in storage before dropping off house keys and checking in to the motel. The storage of choice is a dingy abandoned dump, the best Ipswich can offer. It's secure enough to put our belongings there.

Shame surrounds me, pulling up to the motel. Unlike the Hitchcock film, all the rooms are occupied in this motel. Here to witness a family. An African family with nowhere to go.

Another superpower of my mother's is being a magician using misdirection. You think there is something going on, no—keep moving, nothing to see. It's also impossible to lie to her and get away with it. She does have the memory of an elephant. I rock up to the motel, greeted with all smiles, as if there are cameras around.

Angel, my closest sibling in age, is as diplomatic as our mother. On this issue of temporary homelessness, she surprises me when she leaves a review of the real-estate agency handling our house hunt, calling them racists. Jared from the agency calls me after Angel posts it online. As I am a reference on the application, I speak to him. I candidly tell Jared I don't know nothing about that, which is a lie. I am getting a kick out of this. He is nervous, panicking for a feeling of maybe being racist. I tell Jared I will speak to Angel to consider taking the review down if they could get us a few inspections. Until then, I put up a no-good fight, no fight at all. I let them have this dogfight out in the open. It's riveting stuff.

But it feels like Malawi all over again. It feels like seeking asylum all over again. Struggle, poverty, one room. The camp. A hut. Motel room. One. All of us in it. Fuck this, I get my own accommodation. I feel selfish, but what they are doing feels self-inflicted, and I hate it. Is that the point of being marginalised? Fuck! After putting everything into storage, I drive everyone in our late-2000s Toyota Camry, through potholes, to an unmarked parking space in front of the rooms of the motel, which are structured in rows. I check them in and go to my Airbnb—tomorrow I fly back to Sydney.

In my Airbnb, I put together a list of my family members. It is messy for many reasons. One of which is that my family has different last names going far back. I add Emmanuel first. I was too young to notice the pensiveness on my father's face. A man dealing with how to navigate a world he didn't feel at home in. Who had to lie about who he was. Even to his kids. I hope to rectify and clarify my family history—to reflect a pulchritude within our lineage. Seba is an idea of what it means to build a home, an idea wrapped up in glitter. Awaiting Santa to pick it up for God's children everywhere. Emmanuel.

I am eager to put together a sort of family tree when I am back in Sydney. My patience is tamed, though, of my own volition in part. I am limited by how much my mother has told me about our family, where we are from, or any family members left to tell our tale. I've to allow room to fail and improve, more on the communication side. I am asking my mother as much as I can. But she is tongue tied. Observing our family albums, my mother cut my father out of photos with scissors. Is it shame or hate she feels running through her memories? I don't know. I do not wish to irritate her grief further, but I will not deny myself the knowledge that I need. My father has no extra time, and I will not ask him where I am from.

Everything in moderation is the ultimate balance. This is not new to me, it's not superfluous either. Some things I have had to be reminded of. Reviving a forgotten attitude or narrative can be a breakthrough and move things forwards. Survival is an examination of what has happened before, to further the conversation. My conversation with my mother and sisters, I want these dialogues to get better, richer. The missing link always being home, what it meant to us. This can sound better in theory, but practically so very hard to achieve, with my family. It would be gut-wrenching for my mother to sit down with me and have a tête-à-tête about my father, our family.

I am moving forward with alacrity, despite her reluctance to help me fill in the gaps. Upon returning to Sydney, I get an account on Ancestry.com, the family lineage website. I am enthused, and so I begin, branch by branch, elevating my family names on a tree, names that don't sound the same at all. Of places and people that once rubbed off my skin and fresh daily. To run on forward in the wrong direction is a fallacy in living. And I feel like I have been running, I need a detour.

I feel a good fresh start is at work here, underway, in fact. I am hoping for passionate exchanges at family gatherings—tour de force chit-chats. Sometimes at the dinner table it feels as though my father runs an illegal cartel, the tongue-tied hushed tones, a sort of no-snitching policy. It shouldn't be this hard, surely it was never that bad. If I must argue with them, I will. Something is better than nothing, I know this much. The sharp edges around the incisions of residue photos my mother made while cutting out my father allude to her creating an artwork of some sort—I want to talk to her about that. But she will not. I want to tell her we can foster that talent if she wants to, collect the cut-outs, and design a collage, let's collaborate, Mother, you can be a curator, designing our family story.

It's an Olympic relay race: the better all the runners are, the further we can go the distance. I am a lone crusader in this battle of digging my family treasure, a background history pleasure. Everyone is relevant. Duality drove my father into miserable muteness. A double consciousness reserved for psychotic people. I will not stand for it. Sooner or later, it gets harder to assemble and align my family with this. I visit them less since I moved to Sydney. One of us must take initiative, and I guess it has to be me. I am not bothered at all. I am being less indolent and more diligent—the mission to emancipate myself and my family from the body-politic massacre that took place in that rainy season of April in Rwanda, separate the threads, and knit my own story.

X

THE FIRST TIME I GO TO Mullumbimby in northern New South Wales, it's with a friend—a self-appointed mentor of mine. I have had a handful of them over the years. People who take it upon themselves to coach me through it all (what 'it' is exactly, I have no clue, it could mean several things). A faux saviour complex floating above them— usually white, these people. I know it too well. This mentor has a beautiful house near the woods—I should be scared; I will get murdered, and my body will never be found in an avalanche of nature. You can hide bodies in the woods, that's why the count is inaccurate, the geno- cidal count, undiscovered bodies hidden in Rwanda's and Congo's forests. I stay with him, my mentor, up here and miraculously I don't die. I will never die; I will live forever. My immortal cells will be studied to make superhumans.

Greg, aka my mentor, has invited me over for a weekend of stories, food and relaxation. I take walks around the forest to catch fresh air. At the heart of this somewhat small town of Mullumbimby is a city of some sort. Greg takes me to a German restaurant. I don't know why they have one here, of all places. I love it. Greg has got two boys and a lovely wife. On the way here, we drive from Brisbane—hours and hours of driving. He lets me drive, and I take command. I swim in my opportunity right now. I am a racer, and this is Le Mans, hour after hour. I have tunnel vision and I make sharp turns in my mind, the reality being, it's a straight road from Brisbane to Mullumbimby. We are making a stop at a gas station with a convenience store, one of those outback stores where the colour of your skin raises an eyebrow from the person behind the counter. I treat it as coming in to have my tyres changed by the NASCAR team before I am back on the road.

We walk out of the convenience store—greenery in front of us, racism behind us. I picked up Greg from the airport after midnight, and we are driving towards his house. The light is coming to us now. I think I see an Oliver's, a chain of health-food stores off main highway roads around Australia. Yes, I think I see one. I will earn so much money and buy Oliver's and then when people ask me about them, I will say, yes, they are named after the owner, me—this is ultimate happiness. I drive by one of my stores and see headlights come at us from the opposite direction. Time changes next to the odometer—we have crossed the border, into an unfamiliar state. I race to finish. I have horsepower. A hard-core rock and roll—none of that Bowie soft rock and roll. This car is moving, and I am the Jesus behind the wheel. Rocking it hard like a metal band, yes, metal is apt, all metal bands with devil or evil in them. I am that great on the wheels, scary. Greg sits next to me in the passenger seat as if I am taking a driving test, surprised by my race-driving skills—I am a beast. He looks at me, wondering how I became this good at driving and everything I do.

I probably don't need any advice, but he and others offer it anyway. They say, 'Keep your receipts for taxes. Be yourself first and funny second.' Ah yes, the good fear factor, taxation. 'Enjoy the ride, brother. It is like a roller-coaster.' 'Try to follow that, brother.' This one comes as a whisper in my ear. Petty comedians, thinking that show-cases mean something. 'I would pay five dollars to see you do a solo show.' This one I didn't know how to take. The view of comedians is too solipsistic sometimes from both the participants and spectators. More recently, the view has shifted from court jesters to modern-day thinkers, and that's maybe too high a pedestal. My view has always been about the work well done, and perhaps I disregard many of these so-called wisdoms. Yet they keep flooding in. The last piece of advice is from an American comedian, who is white, aiding me to be more animated, saying that I remind him of Kevin Hart. And as far as I can see, it's because Kevin and I are both black.

Two people arrive in a village, coming to do comedy. Villagers are excited and so are the performers. Chairs are arranged and food trucks are brought out. Fees are waived based on populating by impregnation of the arts, what a splendid idea. This is way back in the old days, when being a performer was synonymous with a salesperson. We (the performers) invited or otherwise, often not, we go to the people—off we go, with our notebooks full of premises, and sometimes punchlines. Arriving in the village by horse or bike. To a venue—a bar, a tent, a nightclub or anything with a speaker and mic. After which we wait and hope—for an insertable audience, wanting amusement, distraction, to pass time. Right now, two comedians pull up to Greg's driveway. We arrive on a Holden hatchback, a family car. Toys in the back. Too many things in the back, a child safety seat. I hope they don't expect me to amuse them. I left my notebook behind. His wife and kids welcome us with smiles. The man just came back from the road after all, like a rolling stone, finding its way home.

I am sitting in the back corner of the right side of the Comedy Store in Sydney. Comics sit here to watch other comics on stage. I have been performing at this club for as long as I can remember since arriving in Sydney. It doesn't take me long at all. Again, I am that nice on the mic. They book me to tour with them on roadshows and hone my skills with the country Australian audience—I hold my own. But I always come back to the Comedy Store in the city, the blend of different audiences creates a unique atmosphere. Today is special though, different, magnificent. Anticipation is in the air. Laughs are also in the mix—when an audience is laughing already, before the comedy show starts, it gives it more of an aura. A spectacular line-up for a spectacular show. I shift in my seat to adjust, getting comfortable. Next to me is Aleks, who is coming to support and watch. But he is also expecting a guest everyone is keen to see. Earlier, before this week starts, I get an email forwarded to me from my manager about a special guest appearing at the Comedy Store and thus I am asked to be on the line-up, but not to disclose such matters to the public as they have a huge profile.

Comedians arrive in cars to gigs, Ubers maybe, and most of the time on bicycles—rich comedians arrive with bodyguards. In walks through the curtains of the Comedy Store a short man accompanied by four massive bodyguards. Our special guest has arrived. Aleks, goodness bless the boy, almost jumps out of his seat. 'Is that him? Is that him?' Yes, I think that's him, I know that's him. A Rolex made of yellow and white of the highest carat gold sits on his left wrist. I rob him now and I am set for life; if it goes wrong, I am in jail for life.

I weigh it up: four massive bodyguards *v.* me (who indulges in Brazilian jiujitsu) = jail time for me with multiple concussions.

Brazilian jiujitsu is a de-escalating practice, much like parkour, not useful in an actual fight. I pass on the stealing, there are better ways and better reasons to end up in jail.

Our special guest is wearing a hoodie, and it's not from Uniqlo. I know it's him, so does the crowd near us. The timing couldn't be more perfect. The person on stage hints that our guest has arrived, and the crowd chants, 'Kevin! Kevin! Kevin!' I feel the ripple of his name fill the air and contain it. Mr Kevin Hart sits in front of me in the comics section. I can see he knows they have caught on to him. He yells to the crowd, 'Okay, Okay!' I will jump up on stage. Alluring as it can be, in the presence of beaming stars, they come and go. And nothing is a gentler reminder of that than the surrounding treatment. Mr Hart is in the back area after giving the crowd what they want. We, those on the same show as him, are not allowed backstage. Which is annoying because backstage is the comedian's area. The four bodyguards make a formation ready for the war. A star witnessed from a glance—one goes, and another comes.

Backstage at the Comedy Store is where most comics hang out to smoke and drink. The back leads to the stairs all the way to the emergency exits—they act as an exit for the audience as well when double shows are on. To not clog doors. The first show's audience leaves through the fire-exit and the second show's audience comes through the front door. The middle passage between club and outside. I enjoy coming in through the fire-exit door to access the green room, because of how small it is and its proximity to the toilet, everyone ends up hanging near the stairs.

On one evening, this is where we find another guest act, Sasha Cohen. There is, much like our earlier guest, an entourage following Mr Cohen, partly because he is a character act on the line-up and needs a team of writers to accompany him. They set up a dinner table for Mr Cohen. Wine glasses and snacks will be consumed. The rest of us comedians will loiter around this table later, like crime unit detectives at a scene, looking for clues. Something, anything. This is after they are gone, because no one is allowed near Mr Cohen at all during the set. Word on the street is that Mr Cohen/Borat/Ali G is at the Comedy Store doing shows. This terrifies everyone at the club. They are afraid he is going to get mugged or something. I don't know what happens to famous people. The first weekend show is low key. By the time the second show comes around, there is a line waiting outside to see the man. I think he has a residency here. On the line-up of the show, I go after Mr Cohen. I am nervous—this is the only time I say hello to the man, well, Ali G, the character, coming off stage. He is in character the whole time. Unbeknown to me, Ali G is a gangster and talks like a brother. I walk to the stage after his performance and open with, 'It's good to see another brother!'

First stop of roadies is Newcastle. On a 'New in Town' tour. The acts, in order of the craziest, are as follows, Pat aka beach boy, and the driver of the HiAce Toyota bus we all are in—our safety is in his very lofty hands. Second roadie is Rathy, who is so crazy that he doesn't fall on the spectrum. He is also our news guy, he literally reads newspapers like a British person. He has a bag full of them as well. Then I am up next—I am proud of myself for making third on this list! But then, we must wait and hear everyone's account of the stories. I am the designated DJ, not what makes me crazy, by the way. What makes me crazy then, you ask? If I tell you, I will have to kill you. I bring the tunes and we ride. Blake is next—Melbourne's very own long-haired beautiful blond skater boy, he is cool all right. And, finally, Lauren—who would kill me at ranking her all the way down here, but I have my reasons. The funniest gossips and tips come from her. And this is us. Tight. The Jackson 5. Each bringing twenty-minute sets and Pat hosting shows. We are off on a tour pre-pandemic, touchy touch down.

Mullumbimby is our third or fifth stop. Just after Byron Bay. I remember it from the time with Greg, the mentor. Here, they still have a video rental place with a porn section behind the red curtains. As if the internet has not spread here yet. These are our audiences. We perform to literally two people. The mantra in the comedy scene is 'earning your stripes', 'becoming a better comedian'. All this rhetoric is at the expense of not getting paid for one's work, irregular fluctuating sleeping hours and terrible eating habits.

I never quite believe in this kind of straight-line growth. I have always been of the school of thought that there should be an upward mobility to anything one engages in. One has to start somewhere, and here I am, sad being in this room. The two people watching our show are making me rethink my choices. A lady and a gentleman. I go on stage to the haughty lady, who is apparently on an unwilling date with the gentleman. The man is outside smoking a cigarette, I think. And then he comes inside to ask for a lighter—he forgot his. I am on stage, not performing anymore, but giving a talk instead. I tell him I don't have one and his reaction is that of a disappointed punter in a casino after losing, as if I owe him something. I look at the lady and have this feeling of, what am I doing here? And what are you doing here? I think we could all call it quits and go home. I let out a sad laugh as the gentleman walks out in search of a lighter, followed by a sigh, and say to her, 'You can just leave, you know. You don't have to stay.'

I can see everyone else who hasn't performed excited by this idea. We can just go back to the accommodation and hang out on the macadamia farm with the red dog, have drinks and trade stories while gazing at stars as Blake puts it. But there is life in her eyes after my statement. She composes herself and shuffles to get a bit more comfortable, smiles and says, 'I am a therapist. This is good. Keep going.'

The last stop is in Brisbane. We have trudged through the towns scouting for people to hear our stories. Stop after stop of asking for their attention. We have ended up in Brisbane, my home turf. I feel comfortable here. I am going to catch up with some friends I haven't seen for a while. We are doing shows in the Valley. It's one of the first decent shows we do. I go to see my family. I am ashamed of what I have been doing the last few weeks. I don't invite them. I want to make it worth their time, make them proud of me. I glance at the laptop I have—not mine, borrowed from my brother Rowan, I will return it. I glance at it sitting there while I am at my mother's. I look at it and work on an idea I hope to be proud of. Something I can take to my mother and show her. A play.

At one of our very last gigs, which is part of the Gold Coast comedy festival at HOTA (Home of the Arts), it goes excellently. We are all very excited. The weather has taken a turn to pour so much rain you would think you are in Kigali right now. Part of living from motel to motel on this rock and roll wagon is contingencies. House-keeping will not save you. I learnt this the hard way. I remember forgetting a bomber jacket in Tamworth in country New South Wales. I clearly recall leaving it in the closet. In the van five minutes after departing, we ring the motel to have them grab it so we can quickly swing back, and they deny having found anything in any rooms that morning. Fuckers just took it. Yes, always check if you have everything you need before exit. And laundry is crucial—this is motel/hotel staying 101. Everyone knows this except a Kardashian and Rathy. Our very own Rathy, who has never lived with other people in a shared accommodation, not including his parents.

On the night of the HOTA show, Rathy is standing soaking wet, his shorts are turned inside out and the shirt he is wearing is the one he has had on for days. He at least showers, thank goodness. He has been running in and out of our accommodation to downstairs where the washing machine is. Not only did he leave laundry to be done till the last day of the tour, but also half an hour before our show tonight, hoping they would be clean and dry. We laugh while rushing to the show, Rathy wearing Blake's clothes, looking just as uncomfortable as he does when wearing his own clothes.

I started looking for a way out—a way into the light. I am already away from anyone I would consider kindred spirits. Very few people I know have witnessed atrocity of genocidal magnitude. How then? How do I express the sadness of it all without a frame of reference—without permission? I tiptoe through landmines of sorrows that hover over my family, my nation and my people. I am a lowlife. There are no elites in my family. I am filled with imposter syndrome. How will I make that leap into the other, into a space reserved for a few? I want to create and show it all outwards, to explode.

Since arriving in Sydney in 2017, I worked at all the comedy clubs while working part-time as a tutor on the side. My first theatre shows are filled with unmitigated passion. It's all new to me—fresh—and I see a gap to be filled. I start by going to see more theatre at the Belvoir, watching my first show in a boxy theatre, set in a refugee camp, and I am blown away. I am seen, actualised, a fact that I can perhaps build upon into this world right here.

It's been over twenty years since we fled civil unrest in Rwanda. I want to bring this story to life. Being in the theatre, I am transported. A cinematic world, filmesque, and I love it all, the narrative. My short-lived university experience finds me at the junction of visual and written art. I took courses in writing, drama and film studies. In drama we talked about and tackled the classics of theatre. And this is my entry point. I didn't know it then that there is a place for me here too. More accurately, I did not believe. But now I understand that all methods of story-telling belong to me.

I write *JALI*, the play, rather quickly. I attempt to get it made. The middleman holds me back, an attachment that can be a collaborative process and very necessary. I am not used to it all, coming from comedy. Solo endeavours in comedy move at the speed of light. I am jumping from theatre company to theatre company, pitching the show before ending up at Griffin Theatre Company. Phil is the man to read the script, we meet up for ice-cream like the true gang members we are. We chat about the play, and he takes an interest in staging it. When we finally debut, Phil has left Griffin Theatre as its artistic producer, and a new artistic director has been appointed.

And then the pandemic comes on top of it. All this and three years later we go on stage, finally. I loved making this work, but it was a gruelling process. I almost wanted to move on to other works.

JALI, a one-person play, debuts in an intimate space at Griffin as a re-opening show after the pandemic. We end up selling out the initial two-week season. We get it extended for more shows.

I love being in this play. The lights, and sounds. Everyone who has been involved in it has done marvellous work. It's more than theatre or comedy, and maybe, just maybe, it is the in-between, that feeling all too familiar to the displaced, the asylum seekers, the feeling of waiting in limbo.

One of the longer stops for the *JALI* tour is in Western Australia. First in Perth and then in regional towns, this is probably my favourite run of the play. As the tour progresses, with the aid of Minderoo Foundation, into regional towns, after performing at State Theatre Centre in Perth we end up in Karratha, one of the hottest places in Australia. You can see the waves of humidity in the air. You can also see and hear flies buzzing all around you. All along with me trying to smack them down. The highlight of doing the shows has been the Q&As. They revitalise me. 'How is your mother?' a concerned lady always asks. 'Still in Ipswich,' I say.

My girlfriend Maali is in Western Australia with me and sees the play for the first time. In Perth I attend the Western Australia Academy of Performing Arts (WAAPA) and run workshop scenes with performing arts students. I am grateful for the opportunity.

'Oliver, you came out of isolation and the first thing you do is go to prison?' Jeanne says as we drive to WAAPA in the Perth Festival Volkswagen grey hatchback.

'I didn't go to prison,' I say.

'How long were you in iso anyway?' she asks, now chuckling.

'Two weeks,' I say. 'I thought I was going to the Roundhouse.'

She is not looking at me now, she is checking both sides of the road like a chicken before taking a left. In a few minutes I will meet the performing arts students and chat to them about monologues. Perth Festival is presenting *JALI* here and they are working on monologues in their arts program now.

'The Roundhouse is a prison. An old prison,' Jeanne says.

'I know that now after being there. But, fourteen days of quarantine isolation at Adina Hotel is prison,' I say.

'You know where you should have gone?' she says, enthused. 'Kings Park! It's bigger than Central Park in New York!'

As the more perceptive of you are aware, there are fundamental differences between New York and Perth. To compare the aesthetics of the two is preposterous. I would stay within Australia for the game of 'compare the park', and if Jeanne had said Kings Park was bigger than Hyde Park in Sydney, I would have been all on board. But scepticism runs through my mind now as she is pulling up to the parking lot of WAAPA. I keep my critical thoughts on parks to myself. I will visit Kings Park and see for myself.

I am nervous stepping out of the car on this sunny, beautiful morning. WAAPA is a notable arts conservatory, and I am a dropout. I should have no business being here, and yet here I am. The weight of this workshop sinks in as my feet touch the ground. I inhale and exhale, deeply believing I should be here, and I am. I walk to meet ten to fifteen students on the grass in a park. My shoulders are bouncing with each step like an Ethiopian dancer, shaking off the nerves.

On the grass the students have prepared their monologues, and we are waiting for the theatre to be ready for use so they can present them one by one. We introduce each other, some of them have seen *JALI* earlier this week when it opened at the State Theatre Centre. I am glad, this makes my work here a little easier.

The theatre is ready and off we go. Inside is an intimate space of maybe two hundred seats.

I perform an excerpt of *JALI* so they can feel comfortable. On the grass, we did some icebreakers and vocal warm-ups, and I feel like they are ready. I also got insights into their projects, as they went around sharing their ideas. I walk to the stage with confidence, telling them to imagine the lights and music since I don't have the full production here. And then it's their turn, one by one wonderfully showcasing their work. I feel lucky to witness their monologues and aid them in a direction of making better work. My imposter syndrome walked out as soon as those students stepped on stage. They are so intelligently involved in their own work. It makes me proud to be part of their cohort.

Next time I see Jeanne is on a boat. Perth Festival has organised a boat party here and just assumed I can swim.

I tell Jeanne I did go to Kings Park, and while I have never been to New York I doubt Central Park is as hilly as Kings Park, which is a peak journey to get to. At its climax, Kings Park offers rewards of a tourist gift shop, a cafe and a playground. Again, not quite meeting the 'compare the park' facts I have heard about Central Park.

At the boat party, I relay all this cordially to her and she laughs. I get introduced to other artists at the festival. I fill them in on my other two workshops on top of WAAPA.

After Perth I take *JALI* to regional Western Australia for an experience of the true outback.

Words, words, words—first it is written and then it comes to be. Genesis and here I am. I started reading as soon as I could. I love a good story. A well-written story is magic. I've gone to over ten schools in my upbringing, moving from place to place. My entire education experience, scattered like fine done scrambled eggs. It leaves my brain with gaps of what I understand and what I can hold. Still, I flock to stories. I am so eager as a child to learn about everything anyone can teach me to mould me into a writer, a storyteller. After we flee when I am four years old, everything henceforth I forge with fortitude. The schools I went to that demanded fees and my mother could not come up with the money before the deadline—it's all now paying off.

A generation has been lost for me to get here, and I don't mean that in a 'distant ancestors' way, though yes that too. But I am talking about people I know. Working too hard. Fathers worn down by the stress—never taking a much-needed vacation, much-needed rest. How to stay and keep going? I feel out of place, missing something, and it's not my fault—even if the feelings never go away.

When a teacher at TAFE tells me not to raise my hand a certain way, that it offends him that when I flick my finger to get his attention, his whiteness feels belittled, lowered to a dog, I act like the better man. He doesn't know how I got here.

Or when the police officer asks for my ID when I am not even driving, I oblige. He doesn't know how I got here. As if that's going to stop me.

Or when a rich white girl in my drama class tells me that's not how to 'act'. She and her attitude don't know how I got here.

My gifts, and I dwell on them often these days, are in the realm of sharing. Sometimes to a fault. I am noticing things. The way my father lit up around his friends. The way my mother lights up around her friends. My parents gave me a gift, to conjure worlds in words. I am a wordsmith, after all. This somehow goes back and forth. Being an asylum seeker is sometimes a one-way street, one that demands you never look back. I don't mean to paint an absolutist picture, but people spend lifetimes in camps and detention centres. Refugees cross the border without looking back and keep going, to the destination, the place of safety. I look back. And I see just as much back there as I do when looking into the future—much beauty.

My sisters are proud of me. It is easier to explain youthful pursuits to them compared to our mother. They are proud of what I have made of myself. All my sisters have stuck with school to its conclusion, so what do they know? Jo will FaceTime me and we will chat about this. She is doing nursing at university. She always wants to show me her braids, outfits, and her new hobbies. A mini me if you will. Smart and funny. An incredibly kind person. She says of a friend, whose shoulders she stood on during cheerleading practice, 'I kicked off her glasses because she deserved it.' I am cracking up. 'She had it coming,' Jo adds, amid my laughs.

My mother is very proud of her as well. Jo is working and studying, my mother always says. It sounds simple of my mother, her aspirations, to wish good health and a happy life. But you try surviving a genocide and we will see if you can aim higher than my mother afterwards. I challenge you. Yes, you. I dare you. Pick a war, any war. But you will not, you coward. Even this, you will not aim at, you disgust me.

Jo came to visit me recently in Sydney, and she is a bundle of joy. A spacy bouncing balloon that is up for a chat all the time. Yes, she is a tarot-card reader, how did you know? She has an old habit, inherited from my mother, of hiding things. My mother, till this day, will go around, whether in my room or my sisters' and hide things, only to reveal them later, presenting them as items she has found and wants a medal for finding. Jo, inspired by this affliction, makes the Apple TV remote disappear—poof, nowhere to be found. Only to reveal a few hours later that she found it near her bed.

If I have made an impression on my sisters, it is to do what they love. And doing it to the maximum. I love seeing them happy. We have been through a lot together. I try not to lose sight of this. Them and their joys give me life. Angel, my sister, is beautiful. She is the older sister that Jo deserves. She works hard. She bounces from job to job. Recently, a modelling agency told her they can't sign her because her arse is too big. We all laugh at the table during lunch when she shares this.

And Boni is lovely. We used to be terrified of her heading off, of losing her in a way and her being incapable of finding home. She got lost before many times. She is all grown up now and her disability not as encumbering as I once viewed it. She left the house recently and my mother thought she had run away again because of her impulsiveness. But no, she just went to the park to play.

My mother puts photos of me and my siblings on her social accounts online to show how proud she is of all of us. We are in rotations of 'Oh, is that Angel graduating?

She looks beautiful,' and 'Oliver is on TV! What a wonderful son you have.' At the end of the extensive *JALI* tour I give her a poster of me mid-show. She is proud and I know it. Most people ask me, has your mother seen this and that? What does your family think of this and that? It matters to me. And I cherish the gift given to me by family, that is very clear to them, and I will always remind them of it. I look around and see the fruits of their labour. My family is in good health and safe with food and shelter around them. I am not sleeping in a bunkbed anymore. My friends are happy and even more gifted, we are good.

The best part of Kipling's 'If' is the endless possibilities. If you can see it through to the other side of the border, with your conscience intact, then the rest can be figured out. Beauty, as it is and always has been, lies in intangible energy, the flow of energy within a soul. My home comes with me to the next life, exile or otherwise. Everyone stuck can untangle themselves. I have seen it done with my parents. They took off the shackles, climbed from ashes of a nation once at war, and raised very kind, sturdy children. I love them dearly and with love, the next house shall be built. Originating from the colours of Kivu, a massive lake still streams; in it I see every single shade. I see a Bantu thread sprinkled throughout the lake.

I slowly walk towards the lake. Feeling the wet cold sand beneath my feet. Leaving distinct footprints and nothing more. Footprints, because as the elders say, 'Wherever you go, leave your footprints and not your mouth.' Words are cheap. The way is richer. Birds' humming is the only sound I hear except the slow, steady flow of water in the lake.

There is an elder with open arms standing in the middle of the lake. Welcoming me to the ceremony, a crossing over of the border. A cleansing of my body. Before stepping into the water, I take one look back at the crowd behind me, concern written all over their faces.

I look intensely into the water before that first step. My reflection looks unreal—maybe it's the all-white clothing I am wearing. Long-sleeve shirt and long baggy pants. Baptism clothing, is this a baptism? I am not sure. A drop of rain hits my shoulder and the next one hits my reflection to make disappear what was written in water. I look up and the elder invites me to come in.

Their eyes are intensely inviting—trust, they scream. You would think it is not possible to step into the same lake twice. And if I may paraphrase an understanding, 'The meaning of the river flowing is not that all things are changing so that we cannot encounter them twice, but that some things stay the same only by changing.'

This first step I take feels familiar. This is Lake Kivu, I realise. Or perhaps remember. Am I remembering or dreaming? I came to life near these waters. I know the direction the wind takes the water.

The lake is a border, between my roots and my branches. Between who I am now and who I will become later. I am getting deep in the water, the white clothing I am wearing changes to mud, the colour of the lake. How can something so dirty be cleansing? I reach out to the elder and they grab my hand. The crowd behind me, wearing all white as well, say in unison, 'Reborn! Reborn!'

I don't remember being born. How can I be sure I am about to be reborn? Baptism is forgiveness, but I don't remember what I did wrong or when I lost my innocence. The erosion of purity from my past life. The elder says, 'Be born again, child,' and I close my eyes. I feel my body slowly sink deep into the water. I feel the elder's right arm resting at the back of my head and their left beneath my knees.

My eyes are closed. I sense how big the hands of the elder are. I am a child. I feel safe in their arms. The wind blows and splashes my face with water. It's not too strong though, I can feel how calm the waters are. The way they rock my body back and forth. It calms me. Birds hum in the distance. I am at peace and free to not feel the elder's hands on me anymore.

I understand 'reborn', that it is forgiveness. Letting go. I stretch my hands and legs. I feel the water dissolving the border, who I am and who I will become merging. I open my eyes and it's just me floating across Lake Kivu. My eyes meet the deep blue sky, rainy clouds have cleared. I look around and there are no elders or a crowd of people. Just birds humming in the distance.

XI

I HAVE THE CHANCE TO become an Australian citizen after being a permanent resident for four years. The morning of my citizenship ceremony, I wake up, have a shower and put on my blue blazer. I take the bus to Sydney Town Hall just in time to get in line for seating. There is a jazz band playing on stage. We sit in rows, filling the entire room. Sitting in the front rows are believers in God, they make their pledge to Australia under God. The back rows, where I am, are for the non-believers.

I am happy my friends are here to celebrate with me. My family is in Queensland. We applied around the same time, but they must wait another three to six months. Because things in Queensland move a little slow.

The mayor of Sydney comes and gives her speech. After she finishes, we make our pledges and officially I am a citizen of Australia.

One by one, we make our way to the podium to get our certificates. When it is my turn to get my certificate, I walk up the stairs. Holding my certificate, I get to shake the mayor's hand. As we shake, I lean in and whisper in her ear, 'We have met before, thank you!' and smile for the photo. We met at a fundraiser at Luna Park where I performed, but she obviously does not remember because many people attended. To her, it must seem like a person she has no recollection of has got a little too personal.

When the ceremony is done, we stick around for some refreshments and go to get me a Woolworths mud cake to celebrate becoming Australian. Woolworths mud cake, I am told, is as Australian as it gets. It's been a solid day.

When I get home, I take my certificate and open a drawer next to my bed and pull out an envelope of all my important documents. I stare at the certificate in my hand. A piece of paper that could vanish in flames. I look at it for a few more seconds and then put it inside the envelope with my other important documents. And I place it in the drawer.

Months later, I get mail from the City of Sydney. It is a note from the mayor with a photo of the two of us. The note reads, 'Dear Oliver, thank you for becoming part of Australia, we welcome you to this great land . . . Sincerely, Clover Moore.' And then at the bottom, 'P.S. I remember you, Oliver Twist. You were quite funny.'

I received a text from my mother last week. If you know her well like I do, you will cherish the amount of emojis she affords to jam in a text. This one read: '9 July: Happy day: 7 years in Australia [emojis for the Australian flag]'.

I read it sitting on a couch at my friend's house, Nat, who lives in Redfern. It threw me into the day we left Malawi to come to Australia. On that day before jumping on the plane for the first time. The opportunity that day to come to Australia is perhaps what Tresor and everyone I left behind envied, that I got the chance to take part in something new, other and exciting. I will get my Australian passport soon and the invitation will extend further, broadening possibilities—an opportunity to get on a flight and maybe visit my home, Rwanda.

The first time I hear of love in my childhood, it's at church. Love thy neighbour, the preacher says. Love your parents. I hear it every Sunday, a version of this and that. Believe in it and show it, with money preferably. Food and amenities are welcome too. All will be taken, received—take, take, take. Shield yourself from demons and bad omens with a tithe. And there it was, right there, as early as possible, equating money with love. So, I am not at all prepared for love when I see her.

I am walking along King Street towards the Vanguard in Newtown with the light in my eyes, when I see the silhouette of her posing, or maybe standing is a better way to put it. She is like a classic statue—a model. Perhaps she is passing time or getting some fresh air—I like to think she's loitering. We glance at each other briefly.

I've been invited to open for a band called Supahoney at the Vanguard, whose drummer I know, or he knows me—I don't know where from exactly. After Ciaran has introduced me to the other band members, I step on stage, only to lock eyes with her. She is a posing/standing/loitering, and now sitting, beauty eating chips. I perform for a little less than half an hour, telling a few stories, and she laughs. The first time I see her smile, I love it. It should be said that other people were laughing as well during the show. I don't want any of you walking away thinking I can only make one person laugh.

Afterwards I leave, intending to have dinner with a friend I haven't seen for a long time, but outside, there she is again. Less a stranger this time around. I can see her with some other people, smoking. She is even better in person, cool and full of zest. She compliments my set and asks what I am up to. I tell her I have dinner plans, but that I might come back. I will come back for a chance with you—I don't say that though, I play it cool. But I do exactly that—come back to see her: Maali. After a good show from Supahoney we go and get drinks, and a few messages later, we are hanging out.

Two days later I sit in the back of an Uber, staring at my phone. I am buzzing after being at a party throughout the night. I duck out early to speak to her on the phone. We are playing it by ear. No proper plans set (difficult for me because I am a master planner), but I leave the party nonetheless—I go to meet her. In this Uber I ooze excitement, energy personified. She stands outside a club with her friend who is doing a DJ set tonight. Afro beats and grime are what's playing from the speakers, hearing this as we make our way underground, our voices thinning out. I dance with her for a bit and offer to get us both a drink. We go to the bar, then continue to dance. Even angels don't move the way she does on the dance floor. Her thick thighs waving, transporting me to a place where I can see the colours of Kivu—the life in me. Her colour reminds me of a countryside blue sky, clear visions of what's ahead. She is by far the most beautiful person I know. Born and raised in Brazil around the water, she is my lady of the Nile, and she tells me, 'I love the different textures of water,' which sounds so sublime, don't you think? The shape of water. Being with her, I understand what Adele was singing about all those years. I have never felt so alive, electric, ecstatic. We groove till late and take a walk. It's cloudy but I don't care. I also seem to not care that I have work tomorrow. By tomorrow I mean today, we have stayed out till 5 am. I am gazing into her beautiful eyes, smiling.

After I've known her for a month all I want is her sweet touch. Even when I am in Melbourne, watching a tennis match, and she is in Sao Paulo, all I can think of is her. Ash Barty plays one of her last tennis games in the semi-finals of the Australian Open against the American Madison Keys, and it is a good match, but I walk out and call Maali. The chilly breeze of Melbourne is passing my lips as I say, 'I love you too' to the phone and let it wash over me, us. I loop Melbourne streets with her tender voice in my ear.

Shortly after my twenty-sixth birthday, my mother tells me this is a good time to think about stacking grandchildren for the family. The day she meets Maali, we are nervous. I have not told Maali about the stacking of grandchildren, but perhaps unwisely I have mentioned that my family is judgemental. And they are. The devil would get roasted at my family's dinner table. Their judgement knows no bounds. I am talking judge and jury in the purest form. I tell her because I would not like to send her in there blind. Nor would I want to be sent blind into hers. Maali comes from a family that is strict—very protective of her. And you can see it in the way she carries herself, she is cautious. We arrive in Ipswich. Still the only place my family has lived in all their years of being in Australia. They greet her as they greet everyone else, warm but quiet. My mother tries, to no avail, to call her by her actual name, but it's foreign to her ears. It's comical.

On a winter afternoon in Melbourne, Maali holds my hand as we walk by the river over the bridge, all the way to South-bank. We are going to a café near the ABC Radio building, we are meeting a Rwandan diplomat here, a fact that would make my mother want to vomit—her mistrust of anyone from Rwanda is special. I honestly don't think she trusts me and my sisters. Now, after returning to Ipswich, she warns me not to eat at restaurants when I am there and again that 'Rwandan people are not to be trusted!' And I'm like, we are Rwandans, Mother. Deep down, I think she still believes people are coming to get us and we should be extra careful in these matters.

We approach the diplomat, who is with another person, through whom this meeting has been arranged—they are glued together. This other person is also from Rwanda. She smiles at us, dressed smartly casual, and welcomes me and my lover to the shade-less table (why, there is so much shade there—yes, right there!). She wants credit for this meeting later, a photo, something, anything, proof that it went down.

As soon as we sit, the diplomat says, 'I could tell it was you immediately. I can always tell Rwandans.' He laughs after this. We then chat about the weather, the differences between Sydney and Melbourne. Compliments and advice are given to me by the diplomat, which I am flattered by. And then he says he has heard that I am Hutu, through an interviewer at the ABC, who I chatted to about my show. The diplomat laughs at this and says, 'Ha ha, who said you are Hutu?' Belgians and Germans. I give him an answer about getting it from my father. In all its freedom and limitations, I inherit it all, and so do my sisters, all three of them. Emmanuel knows about his future. Everything he had to do was under the umbrella of Hutu. The way he talked, and supposedly his choice of a partner. But he chooses my mother and now must relay the message to me and my siblings. Keep going no matter what. This answer does not satisfy the man.

Sitting next to this diplomat, I listen all the way to the end of his monologue. Doing solo performances, I know it feels great to have an audience. He hits every word carefully. I assume he delivers this to every Rwandan youth he meets. The gist of it is to work hard, just like he did in the UK to earn his position and visit home—which I think he has to say because of his title.

I purchase tickets for flights from London to Kigali and go see my family for the first time in over twenty years. London is a great city. I have come here to flex my blue passport, golden embossed in and around the cover. I want to laminate it. I laminate everything, even toilet paper— all things are art to me. Also, if you love eavesdropping (the art of listening) on random conversations of people, then London is your city. It's not a prerequisite or the only thing to do here—there is much to be experienced and lots of wonders to dip oneself in—but I cannot help but be fascinated by the accents; I spend most of my early days here eavesdropping. They offer plenty in both worlds of random (a guy teaching medieval texts) and conversations (I cannot make out what they are saying half the time, the former random note is a deduction based on the person's outfit).

I come over here on the week of the Queen's death and a holiday is declared shortly after. I tell my Australian friends that the United Kingdom has lost a Queen but gained a King, not Charles but Oliver Twist. Kanye West also weighs in on her death and goes on social media (his best friend) and declares, 'I get it, London. I lost my Queen too.' My brother is not handling divorce well.

The vibrant theatre scene here is exciting and the proximity to home, in Kigali, makes me happy. I take steps around the city like a man landing on the moon. I enter Tubes that are basically ovens—whoever complained of the coldness of London has never taken the underground trains, it's a sauna down there. I am hoping to familiarise myself with this alien accent and way of life. A way of life I will surely adapt to. I come here with my blue Australian passport, and I am the best human. A refugee with a passport, I will take back what was taken away from me, my ability to travel. I am ruthless in my approach. I see homeless people near Piccadilly Circus in the foetal position begging for money and I ignore them, jump over them. I conclude in my judgement that they will be fine because they are one Google search away from a house. There are children suffering in Africa, why would I help you before them? Look at me, I am African, do you see my features? Look at me, damn it. I am young, youthful, beautiful. I am a young, youthful, beautiful African and black. Honour me, I will blow my money on aesthetics, I don't care—London is aesthetics. In my mid-twenties, my skin is glowing. And I grow, and to mention (again) blow, with it. It being 'Process'. This is mine, soaking it all in, being a version of me with a passport, transport, means of getting here, and there—anywhere. Do you hear my diaspora voice, the voice of my generation, lost in transit? I bet you wish you could be me. Pick a war.

When I step out of Heathrow Airport and get into the beetle-shaped taxi London is famous for, I get comfortable with my green sulfate (chartreuse) North Face duffle bag. The back of the taxi is roomy, I can see why that porno category of London cabbies is popular. It's a stage back here and I use it too. Slow down now. I tell the cabbie my story, that's all. I vomit my origin story, give him like I am giving you, my story, my trauma, would you like to be me now? I dare you—pick a war, any war, really. I am done with my genocide story, like a fresh graduate, I have no use for old text, old stories. Go and run with it, like you are on a deadline, tell your friends. I tell the cabbie this, and now you. Tell everyone, anyone who will listen to my voice, my young, youthful, beautiful black diaspora voice.

The Queen's death has brought her diehard fans out of basements and English farms. The palace in which her casket lies for viewing (Buckingham Palace), near a park which might as well be called Queens Park, is full of people who are hoping to see the body (being paraded around as treasure). A lot of those in the queue are from parts of the UK that Londoners rarely visit. I walk past the huge lines. There is a gloom in the air and yet people are happy standing for hours—waiting to say goodbye to a tormenter of lots of colonised places, including Australia.

I walk and pass the ridiculous-looking police with their pointy helmets and wonder about their role around the Kingdom. Making my way to Piccadilly Circus. Enormous crowds make me zero-in on conversations as I am side-stepping Londoners on their way to other parts of the city, but I don't want to lose my tail. My tell.

A closing moment: in a car park at a supermarket that is not terribly busy, even on a Sunday, I am on the phone with my mother, and she is emotional now. Perhaps the first time I am hearing her close to tears—she is not what you would call an emotional woman at all. My mother will hold stern a position of deteriorating effect because she thinks she is right, she gets proactive about supermarket items more than anyone I know, she will haggle with anyone about the cheapest of things—so it's no surprise perhaps that she has weekly Aldi catalogues. So, when she cries, I am confused—have prices for an international phone call really dropped that much? But then again, I get it, albeit a delayed understanding, like a satellite capsule message. It's been over twenty years now and I'm about to meet her sisters—my aunties—for the first time. I am in Kigali, Rwanda. It is rather the most beautiful place, and I embrace this intense home visit.

I am trying to meet my aunties. Auntie Shema is the youngest of my mother's siblings and therefore can communicate with me in English. Before being on the phone with Mother, I am talking to Auntie Shema, barely containing my excitement and her barely holding hers as well. I am in the parking lot, and they went to the wrong Simba Supermarket. Kigali is a small city and on its way to super-highway development. There is but one Simba that they know—the original, which is where they are. After realising I am at a different one, they walk towards me now, through the maze. Kigali is a hectic city—street vendors are everywhere. On a tour myself, I dodge a fake iPhone offered to me. Someone else asks if I want to exchange money. There is an impromptu motorcycle-union protest. A musician on top of a shiny green vintage car stops traffic to shoot a music video guerrilla style.

My mother is emotional on the phone as they approach me. I am wearing blue jeans and a purple shirt. I told my mother to let her sisters know what I look like: young, youthful, beautiful and black, so they can spot me. Now over the phone she describes what they look like, and it doesn't take long to see the God-given beautiful resemblance. Auntie Shema to Auntie Agnes and Mama Henriette, they all wave at me. They see me and recognise me immediately. I don't want to hang up on my mother, weirdly. As they approach, she gets even more emotional, but eventually I do hang up and get welcomed.

We are inside Simba, sitting by the café. All smiles around our table. And it strikes me how much I needed this. I missed this. A complete person is, in fact, attached to this. An extended family, and mine has just been delivered back to me. On this table. Cousin Tete joins us as she speaks English well. There are so many things I want to ask them, so much has changed. Yet it is all very familiar. Their smiles covering cheek to cheek are exactly like my mother's, and I am grateful to see it in person. Tete says they are photocopies of each other and it's true.

After trading stories of home they show me around. We get into my rental Toyota Rav4 and go on a road trip. We drive to Notre Dame, where Mother went to school. An all-girls school. Everyone in the car but me would be allowed inside. It's a prestigious school and only my mother of all her sisters got in. Boarding there, she must have moved from Cyangugu to Kigali. We then go to Tete's house, where we are welcomed with Coca-Cola, and the stories continue. I meet more family members.

The last stop is my mother's older sister's house. She owns a beautiful fortress with half-pink and half-grey walls that shine in the hilly suburb of Gisozi. She welcomes us and we have more Coca-Cola. Even more cousins are spread towards me. I am being paraded around, I feel like a pharaoh, alive. It feels right, not like other times I have been paraded. Once I was paraded at a Sydney hospital, in an auditorium where I was asked to share my supposed lived experience. I am an animal, not being hunted but already caught, it's a zoo and these people (these white people) get to exercise a faux empathy and go back to their lives at the end.

This is nothing like that. I meet the people here and I have a tour of the place—there is no introduction that ultimately hints at my exile. I am here. I wonder if my mother misses the place. Surely, she does. She is in Australia, and I am the first to visit. A fact that sits half and half in her mind. Her sisters want her to come, and she will, along with my sisters. It will be bundles of joy. Women outlive men where I am from. On this occasion, I see it. I celebrate my mother. Long live the queen that is my mother.

I am desperate to see my birthplace, Cyangugu, again. It's a five- to seven-hour drive west of Kigali into the southwest province of Rwanda, so I wake up early and set off, but after putting a few miles on my odometer I realise I've forgotten my licence and must turn around and go back. I drive at a speed of 61 kilometres to make up for time before the roads get busy, and they do get busy. And this speeding, over the normal 60 kilometres per hour, as any Rwandan will tell you, will get you a camera catch speeding ticket. Surveillance is at an all-time high on the roads here—from police to military and roadblock general checkers. It is a military-run country to an extent—so it's understandable. But for me it is annoying and making me late. I finally get home and grab my licence and then hit the road southwest again. It takes a little while to get out of Kigali, as it's daylight now. When I woke up at 4 am to get ready for the trip, I planned (always plan) to make my way to Nyungwe Forest National Park, home of the gorillas, and then Lake Kivu, sardines' town. Driving around, I see beautiful orchids native to my country. These purple beautiful flowers punctuate the highways.

By the time I enter the park, it's getting cloudy, but Nyungwe is majestic. Auntie Shema's husband works here. I am driving through vegetation that separates the border, marvelling at hills—Rwanda is hilly and thus full of zigzag roads. I drive to make my way to the top with the cell tower so I can call my mother and Maali to tell them I am near home. It's about an hour's drive from the bottom of the park. I come across a few monkeys, and I stop and look at them, chip away and gaze at the mist and smoke haze over the hills. A breath-taking view, and shortly after I continue. I turn a right zigzag, an almost 45-degree angle, and I see leaves on the road blocking the right lane—a sign to show caution ahead. In parts of Africa, they are used in the absence of orange traffic cones, and in other parts they can be more than an indicator of what's ahead, also of what's behind, what has passed, perhaps an accident or a funeral. I swerve to the left. This time, it's an accident. A truck has tipped over in the right lane, spilling the cargo it is transporting. Men guide me to overtake, signalling with their hands, while other men's hands transport cargo into another vehicle, a smaller one. Big cars are dangerous around here, the zigzag roads coupled with heavy thunderous rain can be a recipe for disaster. I drive faster, past the soldiers guarding the border that the forest holds between Rwanda and Congo.

I am eager to get to the top, to beat the clouds and the heavy rains. I see how much the farmers love it, but I am not a farmer, so my intentions and desires don't live in these hills. I get past another flipped truck—I am almost there. I take breaks. The kids on the street flash peace signs at me. As it stands right now, I am not Hutu or Tutsi, or even Twa. I am one with the earth, and it's beautiful.

I get to the top. The plan has changed (always plan and be prepared to change that plan). The rain is heavy, I cannot see the gorillas today. I pull over to a café nearby and wait it out. I speak to my mother and the conversation is a fireside chat, alive and full of her reminiscing. It is pouring rain outside. I have talked many times with my mother these past few days. She is joyous that I am here. I am happy I came. Believing my luck and embracing my gift (my passport). I speak to my partner and show her how alive

I feel at being reunited with my family. I feel free, attached to what was once taken away from me, to something I only heard through the grapevine—through a record. As soon as the rains clear, I take a sip of my pineapple Fanta and hit the road. A short drive and I am into the fishing town of Lake Kivu, the middle part of the lake. I pull over to soak it in. This is my town. I once walked this earth. I feel it, I know it. I love it.

I was born here in Cyangugu. The family story legends and lineage don't travel far back, but I imagine strong farmers in my roots—the kind that make you appreciate the importance of labour. It is a beautiful fertile land around the streams of Lake Kivu, featuring various vegetation—the most native of all being bananas, Igitoki.

I am sitting on a chair in a café. In front of it is a museum of sorts, a memorial. A genocidal memorial in Kigali. I sip on café mocha, as they call it here. Delaying what I know I should do—visit the inside. I got a place to stay, close to one of my aunties, which is also close to the memorial. But I put this coffee before the memorial. Bucket-list style. An omelette before that.

After the omelette and a coffee, I enter the Kigali genocide memorial paying respect to family I have lost in the war and my extended kinfolk. I am edgy and yet I feel fine, curious even. I see the weapons plastered and preserved.

Weapons of mass destruction, machetes and hoes. But it was people, my people, that were the weapon after all. Farmers committed the most heinous acts possible. They misunderstood themselves; it's the only thing I can imagine having been going through their heads. The mass exodus of refugees captured by photojournalists hangs on the walls. A group of white people on a guided tour take off their headphones to talk among themselves, make commentary. They marvel at the horrors. 'Do you think they knew what they'd done when they woke up the next day and saw their neighbours covered in blood?'

I want to chime in and tell them, choice of power, or is it the power of choice? Either way, it seems to me, we are and were waking up and faced with one choice only. I would love to hypothesise that in a parallel universe these people would choose differently, choose their neighbours. Choose morality over savagery. Would choose love. But love is a responsibility enjoyed alive. Death comes knocking in 1994, in a game of Russian roulette. Someone is going to die, solipsism revitalised, weaponised. Everyone staying will have to think for themselves. I think all this and don't say it, I continue with what I came here to do.

I am passing more people on a tour. Usually, a concerned mother or father with their child. Come to teach them a lesson. What a holiday to choose. I walk through the history; I know it too well. After all, I have been exiled for over twenty years; I have had time to watch from the tower. But being here it hits differently, like a strong familiar drug, hits with a purpose of revisiting a feeling of high to low. Because they follow each other, always, and vice versa. I know what Belgium and Germany did to my nation's spirit, the soul once honourable and now wretched. I see it in the streets. They made my people forget they are kings and queens.

I see photos of the skulls of children and mourn their brevity. To dare to live, to dare face a killer in the eye. I make my way to a less graphic section of the memorial, where families, I am assuming, have submitted photos of people lost in the genocide. They hang like dried clothing, exposed to a theatrical lighting to highlight their faces, drying them in the process. They are mostly portraits. I admire them with great scrutiny, not for any judgemental thoughts passing down, but for a leap of empathy, to feel through their faces the last feeling to pass through their veins before they were cut open during that rainy season during those one hundred days. Eventually, their blood would dissolve with water and the two would be indistinguishable. I have a cognitive dispute to pick with a colonial mind, an opportunist's plan. It's clear to me there are no differences between the faces I see in these photos and my own. What then is it you see when you look at us?

I finally go to level two and look at the children's section. Downstairs I have already been able to tell which skulls are of children. I can feel my heart giving in already. I can hear their cries as my own. Names like Fedele rest atop their heads on the headshots. Single names only, and I walk through the selected few. I imagine many that could not be identified.

I feel a wave of emotions at the end. As I exit the door at the upper-level section of the memorial, I see stairs heading up on the left, and a sign much like those at new shops saying, 'Counselling available now.' I make my way downstairs. I walk out of the building to the graveyard section. As I walk, I read the names of people who passed. I see names that my family and I share. And I wonder if I know them directly. If I share the same blood. I mourn, shedding tears, knowing that I am the same blood as them. That I do share their name, land, spirit. What is left is made better. I walk free.

I call Maali to tell her all I have just shared with you secondly. I hang up and walk back to the café, take a seat and then a deep breath. I continue eavesdropping on the conversation, fully understanding the stories in Kinyarwanda. As I always have understood since leaving the country, no matter where I ended up. It is my mother tongue. I walk out of the Kigali Memorial in tears, overwhelmed by the loss of lives in the genocide, but also feeling incredibly grateful for my finding a life somewhere else.

I hear stories shared in a distant future about what happens now, how tragic it is, leaving a family in memorial locks—separating children and their grandparents, the way I say goodbye to mine. As I notice it, truth is not stranger than fiction here. My father, like many born then, 'didn't know what was about to happen'. I wish to warn him to leave, but I cannot. I am not. Born in 1957, Emmanuel does not know he is being thrust into a civil war. Pushed through forces beyond his comprehension, forcing him to decide to pick a side. It's not really a choice, seeing as he is born, all of them. The choice is already made for him. Emmanuel does not know when, two years later, civil war breaks. Chaos engulfs him and his village. Tears flow down his mother's cheeks—my grandmother, Costasie (what a beautiful name)—her boy inflicted by pain. Plagued by terrible horrors, thousands of people die in the sixties riots. Many flee to neighbouring countries, leaving many other survivors to deal with blood on their hands.

I remember my father's face, name, hair (lack of it). Let me do a rare thing and paraphrase a priori. 'Walk on water // walk on leaf // hardest of all, walk in grief.' My mother and I have never sat down and talked about my father and his passing after being ill, his abusive tendencies, whether they loved each other. I wonder if they did. I wonder how she is dazzled by him the moment he asks her to share a life, a name—a journey.

He went to the graveyard with a wrong name, my father. I think that if God is paying attention, if there is a ceremony on the other side of death—a calling of names to the children God has chosen, one by one, as if specific enough to know them carefully as opposed to a colloquial list—then God shall use my father's original name. Or call him by his spirit. He will hear it once more and it will feel like a great humorous moment, a call-back moment.

The reaction infectious in the room, everyone understands it, its purpose on first impact like an atomic bomb on Hiroshima, distraction of everyone—a beautiful annihilation, and never mistaking it for anything or anyone else.

My father's father, his name is Cariste. A good name, a beautiful-sounding one, in fact. This has become my family tree, single names mostly. Cariste exists in my family's photos. I marvel at a fractured history held together beautifully like kintsugi, that marvellous art of eastern tradition that puts broken pieces of pottery back together, making anew a shattered piece, usually with gold as the glue. To the maker of such art, all pieces hold equal value.

I wonder if we know it intuitively and I wonder if I do. The weight of 'being', what is lost to get me here, the conflicting feeling of survivor's guilt right next to gratitude—I am thankful to have left. My father and other boys go to war based on another mind's idea. Boys, way too young. I see them shirtless, barefoot, standing in formation, holding sticks for guns in one hand, the other hand with its fist clenched, rehearsing courage.

I got a letter in the mail from Time recently. Telling me, warning me, perhaps, that the future is not promised. The past and the future are often indistinguishable. Time goes on to highlight that I am too aware of it and its promises. In the same way beauty can be a promise of happiness, Time ought not to take a symbolic meaning. Rather, embody a relative continuum timeline blurring day and night, memory and experience.

I hope this message finds you well, Time continued. I come with a message from posterity, and perhaps take it with a grain of salt. I have been mowing around what to say to you all for a while. I thought it would be easy writing to you. It's the opposite.

I think it's best to frame this as a perspective. Mine is that good people around you will keep you grounded. Make sure you meet a lot of them. And make sure you treat others as you want to be treated. I can say that I (we) have come a long way with the help of good people—friends, family and others.

I finish reading the letter and realise time has delivered what I have most ached for, thirst for a story—mine, for names of my family tree to fall into order. Names, of course, are just partial entries for these stories—after all, I can have as many names as possible in life. But a story to hold as my own is rare and beautiful. Timeless.

As an asylum seeker and immigrant, it seemed for a while there my entire existence and that of my family involved a key task of having to define ourselves over and over, telling and retelling our stories to ourselves first, and then to others: clerks, customs, immigration officers, police officers, and even bar tenders. And bless parents such as mine, having to explain to us, confused children born in countries not our own. Speaking a language that home stories cannot be translated into.

It's quite clear in Kigali who I am to my family who I have not seen in over twenty years until now. My child-hood name is Chance (French pronunciation). And I forget all about it until I come back here, and my cousins, aunties and uncles address me as Chance. And then it hits me, almost to tears because it is pure truth. It hits me they don't care about Oliver or even Chance. To them, whom it may and does concern; to them, who it matters to me the most, I am still that boy born by the lake. Whatever spirit I embody now is the same I had as a child—that's my identity, part of my quality.

Berlin's air is thick, gross even. Everyone smokes cigarettes, and those days are way behind me. Germany's winter is alive, and I am here on a holiday of some sort. Amid this air of cough, something else falls from the sky. Occupying the space. I see snow for the first time being here, I put my tongue out to taste it and my buddy Patrick says, 'That's some weird shit, nigga,' and I laugh. He be eating snakes in China, and somehow, I am the weird one here.

Patrick and I are talking on the phone again. I am filling him in on my time here. What I am doing: I have been walking by the fallen Berlin Wall. I went to see Nefertiti, who is here. They took her from Egypt before the wall came down, they used to parade her to the West and East side when those on each side weren't allowed to mix—through an underground tunnel I am assuming. That's a Queen. I thought I should pay her a beautiful visit. She is wonderful in-person, a blessing in the present. A protective glass taller than any normal human height surrounds her. No photos are allowed at the Neues Museum of Berlin.

Of course, during my stay, I naturally find myself in a Berlin club dancing to Brazilian funk. And later I will end up at a Sudanese place getting some food. No one here is from Berlin. We all congregate here from around the world to supplement company to each other. Berliners will be quick to announce their estrangement to anyone within a drinking radius—a much-expanded zone, it would seem, people drink outside here. The city does surprise me with some of the best jazz I have seen live ever too.

I walked through the cement pillars—I think they are cement. They are all nameless, the reason behind the nameless design on the memorial is that people truly get to feel the magnitude of the loss of people. The pillars are of Jews killed in the genocide of Germany. The irony being that Germany colonised Rwanda before handing it over to Belgium—this is not lost on me as I watch a couple play hide and seek between the pillars set on a hilly ground such that I get submerged in the matrix.

I am standing next to him while he holds a cigarette, smoke oozing on its end. I hold his sombre gaze. He asks where I am from, and I tell him. He tells me he is from Nigeria where elections are coming up and he is stressed. It's evening and he is about to start a shift, working as a cleaner—once paid, he can send money back home. He tells me about his desire to be there in Nigeria and vote. I don't share his desire. Votes don't mean the same where I am from. I tell him I just visited home for the first time in a long while. This puts a smile on his face, happy to hear that I still remember home. And I do, even being here in the colonisers' nation, I remember where I am from. Despite all efforts made to make me forget.

Paris is better than Berlin in some ways and other ways not. For instance, Berlin as a city smells (not good), the people have an alright smell. But in Paris, the people smell good or bad, nowhere in the middle. And the city smells fine. My view of Paris does not lean strongly in any direction. Which is not the same as Americans. On my way back to Sydney from Paris, I go via Los Angeles and an American mother starts a conversation towards the end of our long flight. She asks me where I am coming from, and I tell her Paris. And you would have thought she freebased a Coca-Cola drink. Her energy and morale go off the charts, bouncing from 'This baby is the end of my peace' to 'Tell me everything about Paris because I just LOVE LOVE the place.' And Eiffel Tower, love it—will not climb it, but it's nice to look at. I love it as much as the next guy. The rest of the city is beautifully placed in hilly places that remind me of Kigali.

I am in a bakery in Paris, and I ask if they speak English. Now I should say, there was a period in my life where fluency in French was in me. And I probably could hold a conversation or two in French, but I refuse on principle. So, when I ask the man in the bakery if I can order in English he gives me an offended face, spite almost—that French arrogance. It's the opposite that I get in Kigali, I get pardoned for not speaking the language, again, I probably could hold a small talk but really, I do not bother at all. In Berlin I got indifference when people realised I don't speak German, and the world moves on.

On my way home to Rwanda for the first time, I stopped by Egypt, home of the beautiful Nefertiti and many other queens. I have a long layover and so I purchase a visa to enter the country and go see the Pyramids of Giza. I step out of Cairo airport and it's so hot, I feel baked. Plus, I am coming from London, so I am dressed like I am going to dig snow from the pavements. I am overdressed for Cairo. The buzz in the city is electric. I get an Uber and make my way to the Giza pyramids, where remains of proof of civilisation far richer and cooler than the Europeans' exists.

Once inside, I get a guide who shows me all around the place. They are a chirpy people, the Egyptians, and I love my time there. Before I leave my guide invites me to have tea with him at his place near the pyramids—on campus, if you will. I think he lives inside a pyramid. I am sure he is a pharaoh. But I had to pass on the tea, it was boiling hot, I don't know how he does it.

Before leaving Kigali, I had dinner and drinks with my cousin Tete, my cousin Henriette, and her husband. I suggested the Indian restaurant because I had been there before, and I felt they would trust it. Because much like my mother, they are very suspicious of Rwandans, and they live here. I mean, I want to land on the safe side here. If their paranoias are warranted, I don't want to be that overseas cousin who comes back after twenty years and poisons everyone.

Henriette, along with her husband, are God-fearing, and they do not drink. Cousin Tete is up for some. My being late to the dinner causes her to get a head start on the alcohol, and she is a lightweight in this arena. When I get there, I must order a few cocktails to catch up with her, nothing too crazy because I am flying back tomorrow. Tete is hilarious when drunk and we are waxing poetic about her work, ambitions and love life. We order food and talk some more. It's impossible to make up for twenty years of lost time over a dinner. Henriette got married recently and they show me the photos, I share with them updates of my mother and my sisters while we eat and drink.

I hold their faces in eternity now. Tables all around us sizzling with Indian spices. Chatter entering and leaving booths, punctuated by more drinks and more food. My cousins give me gifts for my mother back in Australia. After dinner, I get my driver to drop everyone at their places. Kigali at night is beautiful—you see lights only of small and big houses from the many summits of the city, it feels like you are at an amazing concert.

At the end of dropping everyone off, I go back to my accommodation. I lie down peacefully, remembering my goodbyes to them, not feeling like it's the last time I will see them: a comforting farewell.

In Kinyarwanda, my given surname means gratitude. A third decade is approaching since the 1994 mass atrocity in my home. I marvel at my luck to have been one of few. I feel grateful, to be one that claims living as my own. I do not take it lightly, the pleasures and pains accompanying this gift of life. It is true that sometimes it rains in April in Rwanda, but that is just that—sometimes.

I remember, sitting *face à face* with my cousins in Kigali. I see them as if recently baptised. Glory brought back to them. Once blue, now new. They are filled with joy and gratitude beyond any name. A tremendous rapture ascends inside me. Heavenly, promised and delivered. I am home.

Gratitude

Bismillah.

Thank you to my family and friends.

Discover a
new favourite

Visit **penguin.com.au/readmore**